COLLABORATIVE
CHANGE
in Education

COLLABORATIVE

CHANGE
in Education

Gill Nicholls

**KOGAN
PAGE**

London • Stirling (USA)

First published in 1997

Kogan Page Limited
120 Pentonville Road
London N1 9JN
and
22883 Quicksilver Drive
Stirling, VA 20166, USA

© Gill Nicholls, 1997

British Library Cataloguing in Publication Data

A CIP record for this book is available from the British Library.

ISBN 0 7494 2113 4

Typeset by Kogan Page
Printed and bound in Great Britain by Clays Ltd, St Ives plc

Contents

Abbreviations

AISR	Annenburg Institute School Reform
CATE	Council for the Accreditation of Teacher Education
CES	Coalition of Essential Schools
CPD	continuing professional development
DfE	Department for Employment
DfEE	Department for Education and Employment
DES	Department of Education and Science
GEST	Grant for Education Support and Training
GRIST	Grant Related Inservice Training
HEI	higher education institution
HEFC	Higher Education Funding Council
HMI	Her Majesty's Inspectors
ITE	initial teacher education
INSET	inservice education and training
LEATGS	Local Education Authority Training Grant Scheme
LEA	Local Education Authority
LMS	Local Management School
NSRFP	National School Reform Faculty Program
NQT	newly qualified teacher
OECD	Organization for Economic Cooperation and Development
OFSTED	Office for Standards in Education
OHMCI	Office of Her Majesty's Chief Inspectorate
SDC	School Development Coordinator
TTA	Teacher Training Agency

Preface

This book aims to introduce the key issues in the development of collaborative partnerships between schools and higher education institutions (HEI) as a way of promoting continual professional development of both communities. Although it gives a general overview of partnership and collaboration as it exists today, it does not sacrifice depth of analysis in an attempt to cover every aspect of the topic. Rather, it concentrates on specific areas, perspectives and key issues of collaboration and professional development.

I believe that although there may never be a 'true' collaborative partnership there are, nevertheless, many different aspects which can be drawn together that may facilitate such an outcome. Thus, while not underestimating the problems, complexities and cultural differences that exist, I try to stress the positive and possible aspects of collaboration. My arguments move away from the idea that research and professional development are 'done to teachers' and stress the need to see both institutions working together to produce a two-way flow of expertise and educational change. I think that the one way forward is to stress the need for 'civil association' and the understanding of 'difference' through an equitable partnership, one that focuses on communication, dialogue and mutual respect.

I have tried to emphasize the social, psychological, cultural and contextual implications of the theoretical and practical issues that are raised. My underlying assumption is that collaboration cannot be isolated from problems relating to culture and context, any more than culture and context are free from the people within them.

The prime question concerns the nature of collaboration and its role within the current educational climate, and whether it should be an ideological position to aim for. Collaboration at present is beleaguered by problems and divisions, some false, some true, some questionable, but definitely all debatable. In my opinion these 'problems' or 'issues' represent standpoints held by institutions which need to be contested and reconceptualized to form more adequate ways of thinking about the interconnectedness of the different features of schools, teachers, HEIs and teacher educators and researchers. The most controversial and important questions facing education today are concerned with how different aspects of educational research and school improvement are related to each other, and the role professional development can play within them. At present the debates are focusing on school-based teacher research and the role of educational research. In addressing these issues there are competing and complementary arguments which attempt to provide a creative and motivating environment of school improvement, research and educational change. I feel that collaborative partnership can add to the debate.

Acknowledgements

I would like to thank Pat Lomax of Kogan Page for the opportunity to write this book and her help, support and sustained humour throughout its development.

I am indebted to the teachers of Towers School and Christ Church School in Ashford for their contribution to the project and their agreement that the evidence collected be used in this book; and to Christelle Estrada and Pasadena High School who thought the project and the book could add to the educational debate, both in England and the USA, on the role of professional development in a collaborative setting. I also owe a debt to Canterbury Christ Church College's Education Department, without whose support the project would not have functioned.

My final thanks go to Tricia David who gave me the confidence to put my thoughts and vision into words.

Gill Nicholls, 1997

Introduction. Setting the Context

The whole organization of this book centres on the concept of collaborative partnership and continual professional development and how different schools of thought, specific research and government initiatives have tried to deal with them. First, I will discuss what partnership, collaboration and professional development entail.

Partnership derives from the business world and has found its way into education, concentrating on the formalization of roles and responsibilities between institutions as laid down in Circular 9/92 (DfE, 1992). Collaboration focuses on the specific features of schools and HEIs such as culture, contexts, organization, shared responsibility and equity of participants. As such, issues surrounding collaboration are concerned with the personal aspects of partnership, the routine of daily activities and experiences within given cultural and contextual settings. Professional development concentrates on the continuous process of identification and fulfilling of individual needs to further career development as well as institutional improvement.

Partnership and collaboration are aspects of development that are intimately related to each other. It is evident that there are a considerable number of problems associated with the concept of collaboration. These often relate to the question of how, and in what sense, do partnership, professional development and collaboration relate to each other and the educational environment we presently find ourselves in. In fact, this is one of the main focuses for discussion throughout the book. However, before discussing this I would like to point out three significant and related aspects of the partnership/collaborative distinction.

First, there is a legislative distinction. Partnership refers to different aspects of roles and responsibilities which can be empirically defined. It is important not to lose sight of this fundamental aspect of the partnership-collaboration problem. The partnership framework for initial teacher education (ITE) is laid down by the government, and as such has to be adhered to. The way this is interpreted is up to each institution. However, collaboration is voluntary; and the nature of that collaboration can be based on theoretical or purely practical grounds.

1

Second, professional development of teachers is also statutory but cannot be carried out either in partnership or collaboration with HEIs. This separation raises philosophical, sociological and psychological questions about the nature and context of professional development and institutional improvement. The reality is that the problem is based on the division or separation of the two elements. There needs to be a reconceptualization of what working in partnership and collaboration means. Here, I concentrate in the broadest terms on the possible meaning and construct of such a reconceptualization. Some authors suggest that partnership is collaboration and that this is the way forward. There are quite a few that regard partnership and collaboration as quite separate entities and treat them as such. A consequence of this is a struggle between which of the two concepts should dominate professional development. I suggest that this is an unhelpful distinction which should not be encouraged. I put forward the notion of collaborative partnership. This means that the entities of partnership, collaboration and professional development cannot be thought of as separate and opposed to each other in some formalized way, but that they are linked concepts of mutual benefit to teachers, teacher educators and researchers. Professional development is a continuum from novice teacher to educational professor, which crosses institutional boundaries. It is an association built on trust, mutual respect and equity.

There is at present a distinction made between partnership, collaboration and professional development. Some of the implications of these distinctions become clear later in the discussion. So far, I have implied that there are several important issues that are related to collaboration and collaborative frameworks. It is now necessary to examine a further point which considers the significance of such relationships. These are very closely related to the culture of teaching and research, ie, what it is teachers or teacher educators/researchers do within their own institutions, and what makes them function in that way. This involves looking at institutional structures and the individuals within those structures.

Issues in Collaborative Partnership

In this section I show how collaborative partnership can fit in with the present notions of professional development, school improvement, teacher research and HEI contributions and developments. I then go on to discuss the wider context of such thinking and how it is presented in this book. I start with the individual. Figure I.1 represents a possible framework of professional development for teachers and teacher educators, within the context of imposed partnership.

I have placed the concept of partnership at the top of the diagram deliberately. This represents its present position between schools and HEIs. As we

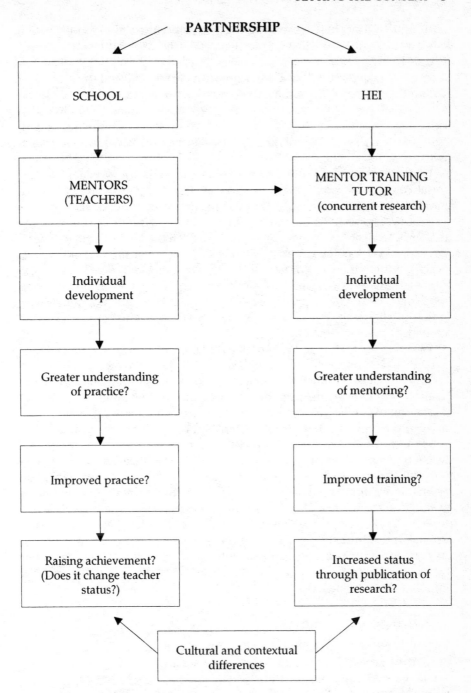

Figure I.1 *A framework of professional development*

descend the flow chart we are dealing with more inclusive distinctions. In other words, I am saying that partnership comes at the top because it 'includes' within its terms of reference the issues that have taken place or have attempted to take place below. By starting with partnership and the individual within that framework, I am dealing with the most basic element of professional development. Considering professional development from this premise highlights the difficulty partnership and collaborative ventures at present have when trying to fit individual and collective needs within one framework.

Individual needs and collective needs are expressed in a psychological and social context, by examining how a social description of structures and a psychological need to construct knowledge motivates individuals to participate in professional development. One could argue that this can have the tendency to view the individual as separate from the institution; however, I go on to argue that development can be seen in isolation and that individuals need the institution to support their development and vice versa. I also suggest that institutions need each other now more than ever before. In one sense there would be no professional development without individuals who make up the institutions, just as there would be no institutions without individual influence.

What I argue for is that it is important to view the individual both in school and HEI as intrinsically involved with each other in face-to-face situations and in terms of inter-institutional relationships. In this way the individual and the institution are never free from their social, cultural and contextual environments and commitments, but have to appreciate and acknowledge the 'difference' between them if they are to construct a collaborative partnership.

I suggest that it would be unwise to ignore the 'difference' between teachers' aims and teachers' education aims, as these are external constraints the individual has to work to, and to neglect these differences would militate against individual and institutional improvement and development. However, it is in the interest of both institutions to appreciate what may be learnt from each other, not through isolated, insular encounters, but through joint activity and mutual respect. Thus, if the teacher or teacher educator is not seen in isolation from the context and culture in which they and their institution operate, an equitable relationship may develop that is neither imposed nor restricted.

The Structure of the Book

The main theme of this book is collaborative partnership and professional development of schools and HEIs, and the extent to which collaboration plays a role. Each chapter deals with a specific issue, by identifying the central points of debate and linking them to possible ways forward.

Chapter 1 examines the concept of collaboration by focusing on the professional teaching and research communities, suggesting that they need to work collaboratively in order to improve each other's practice. Substantive and strategic elements are identified and explored through an attempt at defining cooperation and collaboration within a learning environment. This is achieved by considering a metaphor for working in collaboration. Having set out a working definition, I draw on the work of Goodlad (1993) and Senge (1990) to establish a forum for discussing why schools and HEIs need to collaborate and the role professional development might play. I identify areas of collaboration and cooperation that exist or could exist by considering school and HEI perspectives. The chapter is brought to a close by stating there is a need for a theoretical context in which to operate collaborative frameworks.

Chapter 2 examines the nature and context of working in 'partnership', suggesting that expertise can be a two-way flow, whereby a dynamic equilibrium of professional interchanges is created. It defines partnership in terms of recent government policies and suggests an interpretation of what such definitions mean in practical terms. Through the work of Crozier (1990), Pugh (1989) and Batsleer *et al.* (1992) a perspective of partnership is derived that allows the characteristics of partnership to be identified. This naturally leads to a brief description of the role ITE has played in formalizing partnership agreements. The implications of such formalization are then considered within the historical context of professional development, and where this may fit into schools and HEIs working 'collaboratively'. A discussion on school-based ITE and school-focused INSET draws on the work of Schön, Eliott, Day, Hargreaves and Fullan. The final elements of the chapter makes a synthesis of these works and suggests how and why professional development should be linked to educational research.

Chapter 3 considers the need to collaborate by addressing three fundamental questions:

1. Why do schools and HEIs need to collaborate?
2. What should the nature of collaboration be?
3. What are the likely pitfalls of collaboration?

Through these questions a framework is developed which draws on practical examples and the research of Fullan and Hargreaves as a way of identifying key areas that schools and HEIs need to acknowledge in the design and development of their own individual collaborative partnership. These include ideas such as 'shared leadership', 'shared learning', establishing trust and equity, and respecting cultural and contextual differences. These issues are then synthesized into ten statements that have been learnt from collaborating situations.

Through two case studies, one based in the USA and one in England,

Chapter 4 examines how two differing approaches to continual professional development have succeeded, or failed through a lack of understanding of the theoretical concepts that can underpin collaborative ventures. Each study addresses the methodology used, the model offered, the information gathered and a synthesis of what made each project flourish or flounder. Based on these experiences and a discussion of social and psychological issues, Chapter 5 considers the concept of collaboration through a theoretical framework.

In Chapter 5, I use the argument of structure (Giddens, 1984) to show how social relationships provide the social context or conditions under which people act, as a way of considering and developing collaborative partnership. I draw upon Dewey and Oakeshott to explain 'difference' and how this can facilitate 'civil association' and intelligent relationships. This allows for an appreciation of where the individual fits into institutional development, but also highlights the individual's need to learn and develop independently. This area is explained through the social construction of knowledge (Bakhtin, 1981; Dewey, 1934; Vygotsky, 1986) and the possible role reflection may play in that construction. Using both the social and psychological perspectives put forward, I try to show how a framework for collaboration may be built and used to increase possible INSET and professional development. Such lessons and ideas would be futile if not considered in the developing context of educational change, both internally and externally imposed.

Chapter 6 takes us forward, or at least I hope is sufficiently provocative to make us think about the possible options schools and HEIs have in working together in the future – a future that appears to be ever more closely prescribed by external agencies such as the TTA and government legislation; a future that is dominated by discussions on the value, relevance and applicability of educational research; a future forced to view choice and uncertainty as prerequisites to survival. This appears to be a gloomy future, but I argue strongly that although schools are increasingly being empowered through direct and indirect funding to choose who, how and when they wish to collaborate, HEIs have a wonderful opportunity to encourage and develop relationships that would want to make schools collaborate with them, not only through ITE, INSET, degree courses, but research too. This as I explain requires HEIs to reconsider their roles and responsibilities as well as schools accepting that HEIs have a great deal to offer, much of which can be attained through dialogue, equity and mutual respect.

My experience with English schools and Christelle's experience in the USA have shown that 'communicative action' can reap great rewards for all participants. I am very optimistic for the future of educational professional development. I also feel that 'collaborative partnership' between schools and HEIs is the way forward, and this book is a testament to that belief and optimism.

Chapter 1

Collaboration in Context

The 1990s have presented teacher education with daunting challenges and opportunities. Teachers, teacher educators and researchers must be prepared to work effectively, with increasing diverse learners, and to develop programmes rich in content and pedagogy. Five years of school-based teacher development research has made me conclude that educational institutions have to concentrate their efforts both substantively and strategically for continued development to occur. The discussions in this chapter focus on professional teaching and the research communities working collaboratively to learn from each other and improve practice.

Institutions must build their understanding of the knowledge bases for teaching, creating a more deliberate focus on what is required to work more effectively with pupils and adult learners respectively. Careful and thoughtful attention needs to be given to the design of processes that promote development of teachers and researchers. Teacher development and institutional development (of universities and schools) must go hand-in-hand (Fullan, 1993, p.120).

Strategically, schools and HEIs must learn the art of effective *collaboration*, as clearly the various education stakeholders (DfEE, school governors, HEFC, unions, teachers and researchers) have competing interests. However, the challenge for the new millennium is to find the common ground necessary to build a strong base for collaborative efforts to meet the unprecedented demands on an education system trying to cope with OFSTED, research assessment exercises and quality assurance, as well as educate pupils and adults. This requires a shared understanding of a collaborative process.

There are several bases for collaboration: the belief that effective learning is a key to education, the recognition that professional development extends along a continuum for both communities, that it is cost-effective to collaborate. Within this context collaboration and cooperation need a definition, as well as a framework for discussion.

Defining Collaboration and Cooperation

The idea of collaboration and cooperation is not new to the educational forum, yet it has taken centre stage in the last five years, with the push for partnership following Circulars 9/92 (DfE, 1992) and 14/93 (DfE, 1993b). But what is actually happening between HEIs, schools and government initiatives? Cooperate or collaborate? What is the difference and which do we operate?

The *Oxford Dictionary* defines collaboration as 'to work with another or others on a joint project' and cooperation as 'to be of assistance or be willing to assist'. I would suggest that at present most partnerships are cooperative and not collaborative, although there may be exceptions where true collaboration occurs. Here is a metaphor for working in collaboration and cooperation: two children working at a computer on a joint project – one computer, one mouse and a problem to be resolved. In such an event two types of involvement can take place – cooperation and collaboration.

Cooperation: the two pupils individually examine the problem, do not really discuss the issues of the problem but try to solve it through their own individual thinking, and share the computer. Their discussions would involve things like, 'Can I have the mouse now?', 'Can I move on to the next section?', etc. The process is one of great civility and the job gets done, while the dialogue and interactions are minimal. The pupils are addressing the problem individually but are cooperating in the resource (the computer) to perform the task. Social interactions are maintained at a distance and only for practical convenience, as well as to maintain the appearance of working together.

Collaboration: the two pupils examine the problem together discussing the issues, identifying strategies and possible solutions. They work jointly to establish a means of solving the problem. The computer is used to stimulate a further discussion and alternative approaches. The pupils make joint decisions on where and how to manoeuvre and find their way round the software. Dialogue leads to the joint ownership of the project. Each tests out their ideas on the other and the computer, hence allowing for joint and individual development.

There is a parallel concept of computer use and cooperative/collaborative partnership in education and particularly in the field of INSET provision. One group of institutions seeks to make partnership agreements or set up joint projects without actually becoming personally involved with each other. GEST courses and specific one-day INSET training are prime examples. Schools look for appropriate courses or 'experts' to meet the developmental needs of the school and the individuals within them. The HEI is approached and places are secured for individuals, or 'experts' are contracted to deliver one-day sessions as required by the school. Each party examines the problem and identifies areas of development but deals with them in their own individual manner, maintaining a clear distinction between public and private areas of teaching, administration and research. Schools/HEIs use each other as a resource to facilitate their end goals. They are merely 'willing to assist' each other in the venture – a scenario very often found with INSET courses.

A second group of institutions seeks to make partnership agreements through a genuine desire and active interest in resolving problems jointly. Such projects often target specific areas of the school development plan; a good example is that of developing a successful induction programme for new staff. The school seeks the advice and support of the HEI as a way of establishing effective procedures of enquiry into the problems associated with induction. Schools expect quality and knowledge from the HEI, and the HEI plays a crucial role in supporting such a change to take place in the school by working together in setting and achieving targets. Both institutions see themselves as 'working with one another on a joint project'. Each institution opens themselves up to their private worlds becoming intertwined as the process develops. Dialogue is the essence of success. Sharing of problems, testing of hypotheses and producing alternative frameworks are seen as the goals of collaboration. Each institution knows what is required of them and realizes that final outcomes may not be the same for each institution, but allows for individual and joint development.

The above is the ideal situation and one that needs to be aimed for. To date we still have only limited insight into what constitutes an 'effective' collaboration. Rectifying this requires the development of a suitable conceptual vocabulary for analysis of actions between institutions that would constitute collaborative work.

Numerous studies are now praising the quality of collaborations associated with partnership and school-based work without identifying how the contextual setting of the collaboration achieves its effects. This is an important relation to clarify, because enthusiasm for school-based research, INSET, and continual professional development is increasingly expressed in terms of its collaborative potential.

ITE is often discussed in these terms, suggesting that the real advantage for schools arises from its capacity to sustain continual professional development through the mentoring system. This is a particularly significant observation, as mentoring forms the basis of a successful ITE scheme, and is dominated by the reflective-practitioner theme, but rarely are the methods by which these links are developed, established and sustained within a collaborative framework discussed.

It would be possible to take these observations further by making structured comparisons between partnership schemes and mentor training initiatives. This would then reject or reinforce the notion that partnership and collaborative mentor training produced sustained continual professional development. At present there is much discussion and rhetoric on these ideas, but it is hard to extract real evidence of whether there is or isn't a link. Work to date draws attention to the development that occurs and becomes a focus for discussion. Such observations require more research and elaboration. They also highlight the need to conceptualize the meaning of collaboration in education.

Putting Collaboration in Context

The issue of context and the role it has to play in collaborative ventures is an important aspect of success. Context is an area that is frequently assumed or, worse still, ignored. Central to any collaborative framework is the perception of its context, for it helps shape the understanding of patterns that influence teacher, teacher educator and researcher development. Within the present climate of school-based ITE, schools may view ITE as a vital aspect of personal development of individual teachers, as well as a way of enhancing the quality of reflective practice and effective teaching that takes place in the school as a whole. On the other hand schools may view ITE as a way of gaining an 'extra pair of hands' and increased finance for the school. Similar examples can be taken from HEIs. First there is the HEI that works closely with schools and sees partnership as a way of enhancing the quality of ITE and therefore producing competent and more effective teachers. Second, there is the HEI that simply views schools as necessary for school placements for specifically designed courses as laid down by the government. Both institutions' views are derived from a conception of what it is to collaborate. However, the factors that build into these conceptions alter the context in which schools, HEIs and joint ventures become functional. It is essential to know and understand how and why such factors interact. Collaboration as a strategy for professional development can lead to changes in the context of teaching and researching. If collaboration in ITE is seen as a way of developing the concept of the reflective practitioner of both novice and expert teacher, and therefore producing more effective teaching and learning, a more critical stance of professional development is required in order to understand the changing nature of education. McLaughlin and Talbert (1993) refer to this as increasing inclusiveness, whereby schools and universities begin to view themselves not as isolated departments within their institutions but as part of a learning community. Senge (1990) considers this to be 'the fifth discipline' and refers to it as 'organizational learning'. What has this to offer a collaborative framework? It enables an organization to structure in such a way as to allow teachers and researchers to continually expand their capabilities and understanding. These include areas within ITE, INSET and school/HEI development plans. Schools

may view mentoring, for example, as crucial to the way they wish to implement ITE. This may involve concepts of mentoring activities not specified or
designed by the HEI, but activities that the HEI may wish to research and
evaluate with the schools in order to take the 'whole' concept of mentoring
forward. Sharing mental models through discussion, and engaging in a
variety of tasks that facilitate the development of such models is a sound
foundation to a collaborative framework.

A fundamental problem that often prevents sharing from happening is
that individual voices are seldom heard. Senior management of schools often
decide that school-based INSET or ITE is a way of enhancing the quality of
teaching and learning within the school. As a consequence of this decision
they wish all teachers to be involved in either or both activities. This type of
decision is all too common and does not allow for the individual to identify
their role in such a venture, creating anxiety and withdrawal from a collaborative and collegial approach to the project. Sharing ideas and the context of
the provision are essential to success. Arranging a collaborative project to be
conducted within schools or between schools and HEIs is a good strategy for
getting a project completed effectively. Indeed, the overall outcomes may be
quite successful in comparison to alternative working arrangements such as
an individual taking control and implementing change. Teachers and researchers do have rewarding encounters through joint projects. It produces
useful experiences that are discussed and shared, and help in future joint
work. The major benefit to both partners is that mutual understanding is
achieved and occurs within the context of the coordinated activities. This is
exemplified in the role of the mentor within a school-based ITE scheme.
Schools and HEIs that work collaboratively together to develop the concept
of the mentor through action-research methods, have been able to deal with
day-to-day problems of mentoring, as well as discussing the issues of what it
is to develop as a mentor. This type of collaboration is essential to increasing
the effectiveness of the mentor in school, and devising new methods of
mentor training that can gain accreditation through the HEIs. The approach
can only flourish if the experience is authentic and mutual for both institutions. If, however, the arrangements are such that an authentic experience is
not allowed for and teachers feel that they are being forced to enter a research
environment that attempts to create and develop a research modality in
'collaboration' with HEIs that only focuses on the individual's practice, this
is a recipe for disaster.

Initially the above approach causes teachers to feel vulnerable and less
capable than the HEI 'expert'. Added to this teachers and researchers know
that, whatever the nature of the interaction, their progress will be evaluated
and assessed as 'individual' achievements, whether through publications,
completion of a dissertation or a school-based report. It is therefore essential
for collaborative ventures to make the intended outcomes of the collaboration

explicit to all, hence allowing evaluation to take place against set criteria that are decided by all involved in the collaboration.

This requires us to think of the collaborative context in terms of two differently located structural systems and seeing the scenario from the perceptions of 'practice' and 'thought'. An encounter that is effective through a joint project does not necessarily mean that all participants develop more than if they had completed the work on their own. Goodson (1992) exemplifies this argument by suggesting that we need to consider the ethics of collaboration. Within a 'partnership' or joint project, tasks can be distributed among participants in ways that deny individuals experience of all the component parts. A good example is research. This often takes place in a school and does not allow for equity, the researchers' main aim usually being to collect data and publish their findings. However, equally important is the realization that collaborative work is as vulnerable as individual work to becoming dislocated from what an individual is trying to achieve. This requires exploring the types of collaborative projects within the differing contexts of HEI and school that make the process of a joint project as rich as possible for all participants at the time. Hence a major issue concerns considering each party's needs and rights. It requires shared understandings, mutual appropriation of motives and intentions; as Nias (1989, p.29) states: 'Collaborative cultures require broad agreement on educational values, but tolerate disagreement'.

The school induction programme is a good example of Nias' contention. The school and HEI would need to agree on the broad educational values on which an induction programme is to be researched, designed, developed, implemented and evaluated. This does not mean that a school will accept all the areas the HEI suggests, nor does it imply that both institutions will see things the same way. What is required is a shared understanding and mutual trust in each other's differences and needs.

These ideas are explored in greater depth in Chapter 5, where I stress the need for teachers and researchers to become skilled at saying and doing things that can help build a resource of common knowledge and the capacity to use and reflect upon that knowledge.

Do Schools and HEIs Need to Collaborate?

Placing collaboration within the context of two differing structures, that of school and HEI, the question to be asked is, 'Do schools and HEIs need to collaborate?'

Schools are no longer environments where teachers work independently or in isolation with self-contained groups of pupils. A school setting of the 1990s is one where teachers must have skills that enable them to communicate to a wide audience, plan in teams, and solve a diversity of challenging problems. HEIs also require lecturers to work in teams, to communicate to wider audiences, to research, and to maintain a high level of learning and scholarly activity.

In this context both schools and HEIs can be visualized as institutions of powerful learning communities for all involved. With such a rich source of learning taking place it would appear that collaboration is a sensible way of sharing expertise within the two environments.

Corrie (1995) suggests otherwise, stating that it is easier to talk about the notion of collaboration as a philosophical ideal rather than a practice to be achieved (p.1). She argues that part of the difficulty in constructing a framework lies in its interpretation, indicating that:

> 'when the meaning of the term collaboration is assumed but not explicated, it joins the ranks of many over-worked slogans such as "child-centred" education and "discovery learning". Everybody knows they are a good thing but nobody defines what they mean.' (p.1)

In conjunction with this is the dichotomy between the rhetoric espousing collaboration and the current reforms that focus on individual achievement and teacher assessment. Increasingly government policies have pushed educational institutions to reform along market-based models by identifying skills, delivery of content, teaching styles, effective management, school improvement, research-led innovations and increased quality and standards as measurable commodities. Such rhetoric claims that 'corporate wisdom' can produce a new winning formula for many educational problems (McCaslin and Good, 1992). Yet it has not. Collaboration between institutions can only be understood and evaluated within the context of its use. Professional development is a crucial factor for partnership to go forward; it is important to understand the role continuing professional development has to play and why schools and HEIs need collaborative partnership to sustain it.

Professional Development and a Collaborative Framework

Increasingly we are hearing that professional development and school improvement go hand-in-hand (Goodlad, 1992; TTA, 1996), but is this the case? Fullan (1993) views collaboration as the way forward to the continuum of professional development. For this to happen schools and HEIs need to support each other in order to sustain collaborative learning communities that range from the initial teacher trainee to the professor of education, despite there being a cultural difference. Reform must be simultaneous. This is a very noble concept, but to date has not been the case. Collaboration is very difficult, and little is known about what works and what does not. Documentary evidence showing excellence and failure is limited. Stoddart *et al.* (1992) recognize this element by suggesting that a gulf exists between teachers' and professors' views of teaching, learning and education, much of which are identified by the way different institutions work, often at cross purposes. The problems are compounded by the reward structures in schools and universities which frequently mitigate against true collaboration, eloquently described by Ruddock (1992) as *'Les liaisons dangereuses'*. What is required is a mutual respect of each other's needs and the conditions required for personal survival within each institution. How can this be achieved and what factors influence professional development?

Where does professional development fit in?

Professional development can be regarded as:

> 'a deliberate and continuous process involving the identification and discussion of present and anticipated needs of individual staff for furthering their job satisfaction and career prospects and of the institution for supporting its academic work and plans, and the implementation of programmes of staff activities designed for the harmonious satisfaction of needs.' (Billings, 1977, p.22)

Within this definition is the assumption that the process of professional development is to cater both for individual needs and for the policy needs of the institution. School needs are different from HEI needs but the above definition can be applied to both institutions, therefore enabling my discussion to have a common platform. Investigating choices that are available to institutions has implications for professional development especially if institutions are to collaborate. It is evident that conflict can arise from choice which also influences the nature of any collaboration. Individuals will want a process that caters for their own personal development, where as management may wish for a form of development that reflects the needs of the institution. A clear example of this can be seen in the case studies in Chapter 4. A school which was having to improve in several areas of the curriculum required teachers to improve at an individual and departmental level in order to raise achievement and effectiveness throughout the school. The school's response was to start a school-based curriculum development project in collaboration with the local HEI. This allowed individual teachers to explore specific areas of the curriculum within the school development plan that required improvement. Individual learning focused on subject-specific problems within the context of whole-school issues, thus enhancing the individual's knowledge base within a wider context and enabling all-round school improvement. The school's choice of working collaboratively with the HEI gives a clear indication of the role HEIs have to play in school improvement. Choices such as these reflect the nature, provision and appropriateness of professional development within institutions and the sets of assumptions under which they operate.

I would suggest that before collaborative frameworks led by collective action and dialogue can occur, certain roles, responsibilities and relationships must be clarified and built between and within institutions. These relationships constitute the cultures of schools, HEIs and the type of cultural relationship required between institutions so that they may collaborate. To develop or alter these relationships is to re-culture institutions (Fullan, 1993; Hargreaves, 1991). Teaching cultures have had a high prominence in recent educational research and in the professional press. Much of the discussion has focused on whether there is such a thing as 'the culture of a school or institution', and if one does exist what is its fabric? Hargreaves (1983; 1991; 1995) has pointed to a pervasive culture of individualism among teachers; others such as Feiman-Nemser and Floden (1986) disagree, stating that there is a diversity of teaching cultures. The one thing that is common throughout the literature is that whatever may constitute culture in educational institutions, there does appear to be one, and that it has to be recognized when dealing with an individual institution. More recently, the same arguments have been put forward concerning HEI departments of education (Hargreaves, 1995). Do they reflect a teaching culture or do they reflect a research-based culture? Culture appears to have a considerable effect on the perceived behaviour of individuals within institutions, whether these be schools or HEIs. What is evident is that the interrelationships that exist need to be considered if two institutions are to collaborate. Andy Hargreaves puts a similar argument forward when discussing the cultures of teaching, an argument which is equally applicable to HEIs:

> 'The interrelationships among teacher cultures and the connections of these particular cultures to wider features of teaching, to a generic culture of teaching as it were, are therefore areas about which there appears to be a great deal of confusion, and a lack of understanding.' (Hargreaves, 1991, p.218)

Understanding existing practices of individuals working in education allows us to reconsider what it is to create a collaborative environment that enables professional development to flourish. Two descriptions that apply equally to schools and HEIs are given by Little (1990) and Hargreaves (1994).

Little suggests that one group of teachers works largely in isolation, being sociable with their colleagues, but sharing few resources and ideas, rarely visiting one another's classrooms, and engaging only occasionally in joint planning or problem solving. Hargreaves offers another view: that of the 'Balkanized culture', where teachers work in self-contained subgroups – like subject departments – that are relatively insulated from one another, and that struggle competitively for resources and principals' favours.

These descriptions tend to form a picture of fragmented professional relationships that would not allow individuals to build on each other's expertise, both between and within institutions. Hargreaves (1995) argues that if we re-culture schools (and I would suggest HEIs as well) to create collaborative cultures among teachers (lecturers) with the wider community, the dynamics would be reversed. A climate of trust and pooled resources that can deal with complex problems would be established. This argument fosters the notion that collaboration enhances development, a crucial element of which is the wilful involvement of critics and sceptics (Hargreaves, 1995, p.3).

If professional development is to be a dynamic process for schools and HEIs we must recognize that diverse expertise can and does contribute to learning, problem solving, critical inquiry, reflection and continual professional development. It is therefore in the interests of both institutions to forge links and collaborate. Working together is not just a way of building relationships and collective resolve: it can be a source of learning, ie, collaborative cultures help turn individual learning into shared learning (Hargreaves, 1995). The shared concept of mentoring is a prime example.

Areas of collaboration and cooperation

The significant changes that have taken place in education since the 1988 Education Act have influenced the directions and focus of interest both in schools and HEIs, each institution having its particular perspective. Examining some of the main issues allows us to identify areas of similarity and diversity that may affect professional development and the form a collaborative framework may take.

Schools and HEIs have statutory duties to perform, and are equally constrained by some of these duties, for example, conducting SATs, training of teachers on a school-based model, school development plans and research. Interestingly many of the external constraints on schools, whether they be in the UK or the USA, have similar components such as inspection of courses and institutions, central funding, an imposed curriculum and a commitment to professional development. I have identified areas of significance in England and Wales (parallels can be found in the USA) and grouped them into two perspectives for ease of discussion:

The school perspective
1. Introduction of the National Curriculum
2. Introduction of OFSTED
3. Introduction of school-based ITE
4. Introduction of school-focused and school-based INSET
5. Monitoring of quality teaching and learning outcomes.

The HEI department of education perspective
1. The effect of the introduction of the National Curriculum
2. Introduction of OFSTED
3. Introduction of partnership agreements in ITE
4. Introduction of accreditation and award-bearing courses for INSET
5. Research assessment exercise.

These perspectives appear to be the same in many ways; however, their foci are different. Yet to reform and restructure education in both institutions requires professional development of the individual and from schools and HEIs. Both institutions need each other for reconstruction to go forward, collaboration being considered as the underlying principle. Day (1995) regards collaboration as a binding activity rather than one that separates teaching, learning and research.

Each perspective is closely intertwined, a good example being the introduction of school-based ITE. The change in nature of ITE highlighted existing weaknesses in the training of teachers and identified key areas for development such as mentoring. The context in which schools, HEIs and the individuals within them have had to learn and develop has shown how the nature of the relationship between schools and institutions has had to be reconsidered and reformulated. In previous teacher training programmes institutions may well have been cooperating successfully with each other by accepting trainee teachers on teaching practice, but having very little to do with their actual training. Under the new ITE schemes this is no longer acceptable practice; it seems that cooperation is now insufficient to make partnership work. The future will require schools and HEIs to collaborate in partnership if ITE ventures and the continuum of professional development are to improve the quality of teaching and learning through the educational spectrum.

Figure 1.1 attempts to demonstrate how school-based initiatives and HEI roles are connected; it assumes that collaboration is needed if joint ventures between schools and HEIs are to be successful, sustained and evolve in the future. The central starting point is the school and the HEI; the example used is mentoring within school-based teacher education. The top half of the diagram represents external and internal issues of direct relevance to each institution in their own right.

Schools are primarily involved in teaching pupils, and are responsible for the teaching and learning that takes place within their walls. The teaching and learning are monitored by external inspection (OFSTED), the outcomes of which have to be dealt with by the school. Generally speaking this is classified as needing to improve the school and achieved through a variety of means, most often involving INSET of some description. Overall school improvement is measured through quality outcomes.

HEIs are primarily involved in educating adults through a variety of undergraduate, postgraduate and research-oriented courses. They are also responsible for research of a high standard, and such research is expected to raise the quality of the courses provided. With research come publications, with institutions being assessed externally on the quality of their research and funded accordingly. In addition, the quality of teaching and learning is externally inspected and audited. A combination of these indicates the quality of an institution.

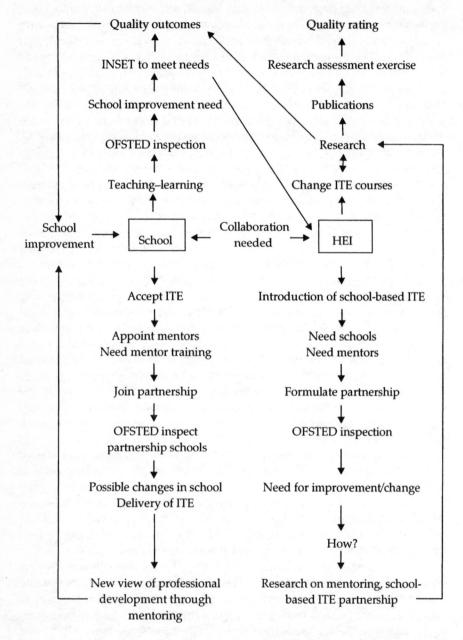

Continuing professional development must occur at each stage

Figure 1.1 *Why we need to collaborate*

These simplistic descriptions would appear to be similar in content, yet different in context. Both are constrained by external inspections and quality outcomes and ratings, so why should HEIs and schools collaborate? In essence it can be of mutual benefit to both institutions. The introduction of school-based ITE is the context of the discussion, focusing on the lower half of Figure 1.1. HEIs had to significantly change the nature of ITE. This required a greater commitment from schools than had previously occurred in ITE. Schools entered the new form of teacher training and appointed mentors for the student teachers; however, the mentors had to be trained, this being the responsibility of the HEIs. For school-based training to proceed a partnership agreement was required, indicating the nature of the partnership, the roles and responsibilities that each institution was to take on, and how the processes of training were to be monitored. The HEIs were then inspected to see how the partnership agreements were working, and as a result alterations and improvements were made. A fundamental area of interest was that of mentoring and the role of the mentor in schools. How was mentoring to be improved? How was mentoring viewed in the educational community and in the partnership schools? Professional development and mentoring became intertwined. Mentoring and the processes were seen as ways to improving practice and as such played a significant role within schools in school improvement. They were also seen as an area of research for HEI that would lead to higher quality ITE and more successful partnerships. Mentoring and mentor training could be perceived as INSET and continual professional development, which in turn could help research the concept of mentoring, leading to publications in the area.

This description poses some major questions. If the above has taken place, has it been done in isolation or collaboratively, or simply presumed to have taken place? Institutions will have faced the changes in school-based ITE and the repercussions that it has initiated in their own way, encapsulating school and HEI cultures. What is important here is the learning processes involved in the example given.

If professional learning and development occur through each stage, as individuals and their institutions are introduced to new scenarios, what are the binding commonalities? Teaching, learning, research and quality outcomes. Research helps to bring about development in both institutions, but there must be a constant interaction between the research taking place and the development of courses and projects to fuel that development. It must be seen as a way of empowering schools and HEIs to make fundamental changes to their practice. Each phase of the partnership needs to be constructed in equity and trust.

Institutional improvement means identifying needs and facilitating their satisfaction. It must also allow for review that leads to constructive action and improved practice. I would like to take further the example given in Figure

1.1 by concentrating on the concept of mentoring and professional development possibilities. For example, successful school-based ITE rests on the premise of well-trained mentors. HEIs have to face this challenge by delivering high quality training. This can only be achieved through understanding the concept of mentoring. Research into the concept begins to place meaning on the terms 'mentor' and 'mentoring' with a view to the possible roles and responsibilities that a mentor may face. Turning this evidence into a format that can be used to develop their own staff before teachers are trained as mentors is essential to the quality of the mentor produced. The process has to be continually reviewed and evaluated, in order that improvements to the nature of the training can be made. It is also essential to further developments in mentors. Their personal and professional learning should increase and evolve as the concept of mentoring is further understood. Here again the notion of a continuum of learning has an important part to play.

From a school perspective, teachers that are designated as mentors need to know what is expected of them to implement school-based training. The basic skills and strategy required by a mentor have to be disseminated to the designated teachers. In the first instance these will be the basic skills to make the ITE programme functional. As time progresses the mentors will require further training and environments whereby they can share their experiences with other mentors so that development may continue. Teacher mentors need to review and evaluate the process they have been involved in for several reasons:

- to develop their skills of mentoring and identify areas for future development;
- to gather information on which mentoring strategies are effective;
- to begin to understand the role reflection plays in mentoring and the effects this may have on practice.

HEIs need to share their experiences and information gathered with schools in order to merge ideas, gain in-depth understanding of issues related to mentoring and school-based training, and as a consequence jointly develop the concept of the mentor and mentoring. This type of interaction requires both institutions to understand the need to formulate ways forward through appropriate action and development. Appreciating the change process and then managing it effectively requires more than cooperation.

If this is the case, examination of why a collaborative framework is practical and operational is required. Such a discussion needs a theoretical context which establishes the ideas of trust, equity, choice, understanding of differences and civility. The types of questions we should be asking in order to formulate an inter-institutional collaborative framework include:

- What elements mitigate or favour the professional teaching and research communities working together to improve theory and practice?

- What is it to collaborate effectively?
- Why do institutional structures affect inter-institutional collaboration?
- What psychological implications are there to inter-institutional collaboration?

These questions undoubtedly have underlying assumptions in their design; they include:

- teachers and researchers can and should learn from each other through collaboration;
- collaboration can occur between participating institutions;
- personal knowledge and process knowledge are required to understand and make the collaborative process succeed.

The above questions and assumptions require a context for discussion. This context is that of partnership, the way partnership has evolved and the effects this has had on professional development, whether it be through ITE, INSET, or research.

Chapter 2

Working in Partnership

Introduction

This chapter considers the nature and context of working in 'partnership'. It examines the view that intentional collaboration between HEIs, teacher educators and practising teachers should be a dynamic way of enhancing the quality of professional development. The approach to partnership and collaboration put forward is regarded as a positive way of providing good, well-structured support for both new and experienced teachers. It is seen as a dynamic situation for improving personal knowledge, teaching situations and the quality of professional development in both types of educational institutions.

The challenge it offers is that expertise can be a two-way flow, whereby a dynamic equilibrium of professional interchanges is created: that of continual exploration, enquiry, discussion, reflection, evaluation, action and support. Teacher educators/researchers can learn and develop from the expertise the teacher brings to the situation, and the teacher can learn research strategies that would help active, systematic enquiry into problem areas. Collaboration is at the heart of this philosophy.

Educational partnership is a contemporary concept requiring definition and discussion. Partnership between HEI and schools has grown in the last five years, especially in the field of ITE, the driving force of which has been government policy. Equally important has been the school improvement movement that has emerged and seeks to work in 'partnership' with schools. Both initiatives require two or more institutions to work together, but the nature of this can and does vary significantly. Do institutions collaborate or cooperate in the face of ever increasing demands made by government policies and external pressures?

The implications of working in partnership are examined by considering definitions of the terms and how historical, social and psychological factors have shaped the framework we find ourselves in today.

What is it to be in Partnership?

Partnership can be defined as:

> 'a contractual relationship between two or more persons carrying on a joint business venture; the deed creating such a relationship; the persons associated in such a relationship; the state or conditions of being a partner.' (*Oxford Dictionary*)

Such definitions give a clear indication that the term 'partnership' derives from the business world. Yet there is an element of intimacy associated with it when considered in a social context, inferring the personal relationships that make the contract operational. In the present educational climate this is often interpreted as cooperating or collaborating within a working relationship.

Recent government policies – especially policies intended to raise standards – have altered both personal and institutional links by weakening old alliances and creating new partnerships in pursuit of greater efficiency, higher standards and more cost-effectiveness. However, many traditional links have remained, though frequently adapted. Schools that accepted trainee teachers in the past still do so, but with a significant difference. A negotiated partnership contract that involves pre-specified roles and responsibilities within the partnership agreement has to be signed. Equally HEIs have adapted in response to government initiatives for change in ITE by reformulating their roles and responsibilities to ITE and continuing professional development to take greater account of schools and their needs. If the provision for teacher development is to continue and be relevant, there must be a strengthening of the partnership and collaborative work.

Partnerships between schools and HEI departments of education have always existed in some form. They have not been contractual in nature, but frequently have been defined in terms of division of effort, limitations and the staking out of territory within clear bounds of responsibility, rather than cooperation (Gallacher, 1995). This has been particularly the case in ITE. 'In many ways partnership between schools and teacher education institutions is an obvious, necessary and indeed desirable relationship' (Crozier *et al.*, 1990).

Crozier *et al.*'s statement is an obvious one: partnership between such institutions is vital for continual professional development, from trainee teacher to professor of education. Constant interactions occur between novice teachers and their mentors. These interactions need to be recorded and shared if greater understanding and further development of the mentor's role is to be sustained. The HEI has a fundamental role to play in facilitating discussions that promote such development and understanding of mentorship. Schools form a central platform for the dialogue to occur. My definition of partnership gives a sense of mutuality and a rigorous set of obligations that form part of a partnership agreement, so how can this be translated into an 'educational setting'? We often hear partnership being discussed as a positive notion and one to be encouraged, but what are we to encourage? The above exemplifies the nature of partnership, which should be encouraged.

Pugh (1989) offers a perspective that lends itself to HEI and school relationships. She suggests that:

> 'a working relationship that is characterised by a shared sense of purpose, mutual respect and the willingness to negotiate. This implies sharing of information, responsibility, skills, decision-making and accountability.' (p.36)

The sharing of information requires a platform, and as such the HEI can play a crucial role by facilitating dialogue and discourse on issues that need decision-making and quality monitoring.

This is a very helpful starting point to a discussion on inter-institutional collaboration. To facilitate the discussion I develop the ideas of a shared sense of purpose by identifying the implication it has for both schools and HEIs in terms of delivering accredited long-term professional development. Pugh refers to a shared sense of purpose; this implies bringing together individuals or institutions whose aims are in harmony. Shared aims, purpose and intent are of no value unless the partnership is active and effective in pursuing and achieving those aims.

Present environments within the field of continual professional development are not always conducive to a shared sense of purpose. Mentoring may be considered by senior managers in schools as vital for the improvement of teaching/learning outcomes, and these ideas may also be shared by teachers and researchers. But, if no time or active support is given to the actual activities of mentoring either by schools or HEIs, how is teacher development to flourish? This approach does not constitute a shared purpose. Increasingly there is an emphasis not just on competition between institutions (school vs school, HEI vs HEI) but the separateness of individual institutions. Such competitiveness has been argued by many as being enforced by successive government policies. Batsleer et al. (1992) argue that there is a competitive element locked away in many approaches to cooperative and collaborative ventures. They suggest that:

> 'even when organisations enter into alliances and partnership agreements, they do so because such relationships have been calculated to further the interests of their individual organisations and not necessarily because such relationships are worth developing in themselves.' (p.49)

There are two implications in this statement that we need to consider. First, schools may join ITE schemes because they feel it would enhance the status of the school, not because they feel it will actually develop the school. Similarly, HEIs may wish to recruit more students as this is seen as a measure of success by outside agencies, rather than exploring the nature and context of the effect increased numbers may have on the quality of the newly qualified teachers entering the profession. Second, inter-institutional partnerships can and often do work on loose affiliations and networks, joint projects and strategic alliances. Consider the possible effects this may have on establishing and delivering accredited INSET courses. School-based accredited INSET has grown considerably in the last five years. The main reason for this growth has been the focus on school improvement, and that this is best achieved through school-based initiatives. Collaboration here has been crucial. Schools have looked to HEIs as facilitators in solving the problems associated with school improvement. HEIs have taken this role on in a variety of ways, some as strategic alliances, and some as truly joint collaborative projects. Each institution has seen their individual needs as the motivating factor in the collaborative alliance. Batsleer's point of furthering individual institutional needs is relevant here. Focusing on INSET raises four central issues which can be thought of as necessary to the success of inter-institutional collaboration:

1. That relationships revolve around the provision of specific services, with the aim of enhancing the service, with how best to contribute and gain from the arrangement.
2. Each institution identifies areas of expertise and makes relevant and different inputs.
3. The basis of the relationship is contractual.
4. The relationship is based on individual members making distinctive contributions in sectoral terms.
   (Adapted from Batsleer *et al.*, 1992, p.52)

From the perspective of schools and HEIs the above foci allow institutions to be competitive. Schools that control their own budgets can specify the nature, type, etc, of INSET requirements and tender HEIs for the service. Equally HEIs can encourage schools to be part of collaborative initiatives that can be used for research as well as the delivery of accredited courses such as the Diploma of Curriculum Development and Advanced Certificates in Literacy, Science Education or Management Studies. In this context collaboration and partnership can be viewed in what McPherson *et al.* (1986) consider to be strategic ways of keeping the educational continuum functioning. Schools and HEIs can initiate joint projects that directly target areas of school improvement, while monitoring the effects of the initiatives for research and school purposes, the dissemination of the results being available at a variety of levels, eg, school reports, governor reports, academic articles and the research community. These reports can also be written collaboratively. Collaboration can then be seen as a structural response which aims to formulate a partnership based on understanding and an environment of tolerance of ideas and practice.

What Characterizes Partnership?

Pugh's shared sense of purpose and Batsleer's foci for establishing partnership form an image of what may characterize 'partnership':

1. Partners share responsibility through working together.
2. Partners take complementary roles.
3. Partners contribute differing expertise but are complementary in their contributions.
4. Partners rely on cooperation, but also on each party being clear about what they can get out of the arrangement and contributions they should make.
5. Partners should have some influence over the partnership's functioning.
6. Partners should have a degree of freedom of action.
7. Partners should have a degree of consent in order to function.
   (Adapted from Gallacher, 1995, p.17)

These characteristics highlight the nature of partnerships that are or should be emerging in our present educational climate. They need to function in the light of more detailed information about what is being provided, for whom, and the intended outcomes of that partnership. The working relationship must be built on trust, an acceptance of difference, sharing ideas and expertise and the construction of knowledge that is of value to all those involved.

The partnerships that schools and HEIs are involved in today increasingly reflect the interests of the government, funding agencies, inspectors and not least pupils in school. A wide range of educational partnerships exist, each influencing the development of education and those involved in it. The two most significant to school and HEI collaboration have been the introduction of school-based teacher training and school-focused INSET. Both are linked and have influenced the working relationship of institutions. It is therefore necessary at this point to consider how the two institutions of school and HEI have been drawn together historically to form formalized partnerships. Although schools and HEIs have worked together for a long time, formalized links are relatively new. Many of the moves towards such formalization have been parallel; for ease of discussion each will be considered separately. A concluding section will bring together the points of similarity that can help understand the role of continual professional development within a collaborative partnership.

The Introduction of School-based ITE

The most recent direct impact on schools and HEIs has been a succession of government Circulars (DES, 1984, 1989; DfE, 1992, 1993a) ensuring that the majority of ITE takes place in partnership with schools. The two most important Circulars (9/92 and 14/93) have provided the main focus for these changes, bringing with them significant repercussions for schools and HEIs.

Circular 9/92 has made school partnerships in secondary education the norm: 'The planning and management of training courses should be the shared responsibility of higher education institutions and schools in partnership' (DfE, 1992, Annex A1.2). The circular clearly emphasized joint responsibility for the development and delivery of training and that both sides of the partnership would contribute to the formal assessment of trainee teachers (ibid., Annex B). The partnership framework did allow for flexibility in that the emphasis expected from HEIs and schools would be different. HEIs would take responsibility for accreditation procedures, certification and the placing of trainee teachers in schools. The development of subject and classroom competence was to be jointly conducted between schools and HEIs. However, HEIs are responsible for developing ITE courses with a firm commitment to producing effective school-based training through partnership. Circular 14/93 compounded this partnership by setting out a 'greater role for schools, which will be best placed to help student teachers develop and apply practical teaching skills' (DfE, 1993a, p.3). This circular reinforced the idea of HEI and school partnerships: 'Schools should play a much larger and more influential role in course design and delivery, in partnership as appropriate with higher education institutions' (ibid., p.5).

Both Circular 9/92 and 14/93 raise a series of issues concerning the practical and structural aspects of partnership as well as the implications partnership may have on the changing roles of teachers, HEI tutors and their respective professional development needs.

The development of ITE and in-service training have often been dealt with separately, but in the present context of school-based training appear to have several common identifiable principles. These can be thought of as the teachers' extended professional role and the source of professional knowledge. If initial and in-service training are seen as part of the same continuous process, the role of professional development can be thought of as a common binding principle.

A good example of this notion is that of the induction coordinator in school. If they are developing an induction programme for new staff, they need to be aware of the needs of a variety of teachers, from the trainee, NQT, to a new deputy headteacher or senior teacher entering the school for the first time. To achieve such a programme and implement it within an organization requires considerable cooperation and collaboration from teachers within the school.

The HEI can play a significant role in the development of such an initiative. First, it can help plan the stages of the process with the schools' coordinator and evaluate the final outcomes. Second, it can offer those involved in the process accreditation for the work they carry out. Third, it can support the initiative both internally through tutor guidance and knowledge, and externally by disseminating the outcomes of the initiative to a wider audience. This type of collaborative venture is a way of enhancing school improvement through the development of individuals by focusing on specific whole-school issues, and rewarding both the individual through accreditation and the school through an effective induction programme.

The implications of school-based training in forming partnerships also require a discussion on the rise of school-focused INSET and the effects it has had on school/HEI relationships.

An Historical Perspective on Professional Development

The James Report (DES, 1972) stressed the importance of schools having their own staff development programmes:

> 'In-service training should begin in schools. It is here that learning and teaching take place, curricula and techniques are developed and needs and deficiencies revealed. Every school should regard the continued training of its teachers as an essential part of its task, for which all members of staff share responsibility.' (p.11)

School-based curriculum development was one way of addressing the issue (Elliott *et al.*, 1981). During this time the idea of schools managing their own financial affairs began to take hold. Local Management School (LMS) 'freed' schools in many aspects, but particularly with respect to the type, quantity and nature of staff/professional development they were engaged in. LMS schools were required to produce school development plans that incorporated staff development and INSET programmes.

With schools no longer tied to Local Education Authority (LEA) INSET programmes, other institutions were considered and approached. This subsequently led to a direct increase in in-service provision from HEIs with schools and HEIs looking to establish working relationships that would benefit both institutions.

A major principle associated with the development of school-based in-service training has been to increase the responsibility of schools and empower them to develop an 'effective school'.

School-based INSET can be, and often is, regarded as a way of meeting school needs while balancing them with the individual needs of teachers (Bolam, 1994). Her Majesty's Inspectors (HMI) have defined school-based INSET as:

'all the strategies employed by trainers and teachers in partnership, to direct training programmes in such a way as to meet the identified needs of a school and to raise the standards of teaching and learning in the classroom.' (Perry, 1977)

This definition, taken from the Organization for Economic Cooperation and Development (OECD) 1977 report, represents a positive approach to school-based in-service training and the effectiveness it has for teachers and schools. The definition is still relevant in today's educational setting, but needs to be considered in the light of changes that have occurred within the funding arrangements for school-based professional development. For example, how are staff development funds allocated? What use is GEST funding put to and can schools support individual learning?

There has been a significant change in the school's role in INSET since the James Report. Evidence of this can be found in HMI reports such as OFSTED (1993) and OHMCI (1993). Both documents indicate that schools now have a much more systematic approach to staff development, with a school-based coordinator to facilitate ongoing development programmes. These findings are based on evidence collected from short courses built on the statutory five training days, as specified in the Education Act (1988), and research reports from GRIST, LEATAGS and now GEST-funded projects, all of which have contributed to sustained professional development. However, very little attention has been given to the longer, in-depth, award-bearing courses in which teachers engage. These types of courses are often at higher degree or diploma level and require teachers to investigate or research areas such as curriculum management within their school in order to develop their working knowledge and enhance the overall quality of the curriculum in their schools.

Personal knowledge plays an important role in the effectiveness of professional development, but has often been ignored in recent INSET courses. A great deal of the focus has been on the 'delivery' of the National Curriculum, as opposed to enhancing the teacher's own subject knowledge, whether this be a grounding in the core subject, familiarity with assessment procedures, or the skills of analysis and deduction. Pennington (1994, p.37) suggests that: 'teachers respond positively to courses which contain a substantial input relating to subject knowledge and readily explore the relationship of such new knowledge to their teaching'.

It is important to understand that teachers need to keep their own knowledge base current and functional. Process is necessary, but of no value if there is insufficient subject knowledge and deductive reasoning to make the process effective. This is very evident within the science National Curriculum framework. The process of science investigations, for example, has been a topic of many a school-based INSET day, yet many teachers still do not understand the underpinnings of science investigations because their own subject knowledge is insufficient. The James Report (DES, 1972) defined three cycles for the 'education and training' of teachers: personal education, pre-service training and induction, and in-service education and training. The report thus implied the concept of the continuum of professional development, although not articulating it as such, in the explicit statement that teachers need to 'keep in touch' with their own knowledge as well as with aspects of the educational continuum: 'All subject specialists will need to refresh and extend their knowledge of their special interests, and general teachers to widen their command of what they teach' (para. 2.9).

Continuing professional development (CPD) has tended in recent years to focus on areas such as management, assessment, recording and National Curriculum issues. Day and Pennington (1993) suggest that the notion of a continuum needs to be understood as a multidimensional process so that professional development can be seen as: 'a dynamic interplay between stages of experience, environment, career and lifelong learning cycles' (p.23).

How can the continuum of professional development be extended to take account of Day and Pennington's notion that it is a multidimensional model? In essence I would suggest that a first priority is to remember that teachers' own personal needs are often a motivating factor for initial development and as such have to be recognized in the type of delivery and the nature of the interaction the teacher is to be involved in. If the teacher can then see or be shown the connection with whole-school issues then the continuum of development may be more successful and rewarding. Day (1993a, p.87) acknowledges that the teacher, 'may wish to prepare for a new role; refresh themselves by more in depth learning about their pedagogic knowledge or subject knowledge'. This suggests that teachers' development which arises from personal needs may be more successful than that which is imposed. Bolam (1993, p.54) reminds us that, 'Professional development is the process by which teachers and head teachers acquire, enhance and use appropriate knowledge, skills and values'. Bolam's argument makes it quite clear that professional development cannot be viewed in isolation; it needs to be regarded as more than a service to meet the needs of the system. He states that, 'in the context of CPD the concept of self development implies that individuals should take responsibility for their own professional development' (p.42).

However, it is essential to this argument that teachers/researchers understand the importance, in building the knowledge base, of the learning and instruction that underpins practice. Mentoring is a clear example of the type of change taking place in education. It requires the building of a knowledge base on which to create a theoretical framework, one that can be used to underpin the practice of future mentoring. Schools and HEIs have a fundamental collaborative role to play in the development of such a framework. Historically the model has been one of theory-into-practice. By this I mean that university researchers have generated knowledge for teachers, who have generally been considered as technicians required to absorb, interpret and then apply that knowledge in a classroom situation. Teachers are expected to show great flexibility and adaptive skills in order to achieve specific learning goals or teaching aims. This type of argument can be found in the work of Lieberman (1992). But building new and effective learning communities requires collaboration. Here again, mentoring provides a good example. HEIs need schools to have good mentors, and schools need HEIs to help them develop such mentors. By developing a mutual understanding of the concept of a good mentor, schools and HEIs can enhance the quality of mentoring skills and the nature of training novice teachers are given. In order for this to happen a new conceptualization of the relationship between teacher and teacher educator/researcher is necessary. There is a place and indeed a genuine requirement for teachers to be recognized as knowledge generators, who can equally feed the research community. Lytle and Cochran-Smith (1990; 1992) reinforce this argument. The teaching/learning process is one that is essential at all levels of education, and for this reason knowledge construction needs to be synthesized as part of a collaborative process within both communities. Lieberman (1992, p.11) suggests that:

'The theory-practice connection is no better served than when it is lived. We can learn *from* as well as *about* practice. Our challenge is to create a community that educates all of us, those in the University and those in the School, a community that expands our relationships with one another and, in doing so, our knowledge and effectiveness.'

Implications of School-Based ITE and INSET for Partnership

The aims of school-based ITE and INSET are to improve teaching and learning environments, as well as to give individual teachers the opportunity to be involved in long-term professional development. Added to this, Circular 9/92 (DfE, 1992) introduced the idea of partnership between HEIs and schools as institutions, not just with teachers as individuals or as a wider professional group (paras 12–14). This does give scope for students, teachers and HEI tutors to have contact with both institutions, allowing for an holistic view of development to flourish and an enhanced view of professionalism to exist. There is no doubt that it can or should facilitate effective training and learning throughout a professional teaching life, and that it is an important aspect of HEI development.

Hoyle (1974) suggests that giving responsibility to the individual for their own professional development is presented and perceived both as a recognition of their extended professionalism and as a contribution to that extension. This is becoming increasingly the case within the context of mentoring. Mentors are beginning to see themselves as professionals and that the role of mentor has greatly improved their own understanding of teaching and learning. They also see this development as part of their own INSET. Such a connection between ITE and INSET is a powerful tool, which gives HEIs a distinctive future role in the school improvement debate. It places HEIs in a position to support the expansion of teachers' professionalism and their role in all areas of the curriculum, through collaborative partnership – a partnership that enhances training, development and the promotion of effective learning outcomes, by taking the role of 'critical friend'.

Within this context there is an implicit assumption that each institution will be actively involved in the partnership and not simply participate. There is a distinction to be drawn between 'partnership' and 'participation'. Gallacher (1995) makes this distinction clear by suggesting participation is a contribution to an endeavour but, because the word is used in many ways, it lacks precision, especially about commitment and responsibility. Partnership, in contrast, implies mutuality and a more rigorous set of obligations (p.17).

Bridges (1993) argues that there is no shortage of participation in school-based ITE and INSET courses, but it needs to be considered in a specific way if it is to be effective, suggesting that:

> 'If participation is to contribute to teachers' professional development, it must be rendered as richly as possible as "experience" ... that is, as something which engages our interest and curiosity, as something to which we bring a sophisticated and appropriate conceptual armoury and as something to which we are sufficiently receptive that we allow it to modify our assumption.' (p.61)

Within a partnership based on mutuality the above form of participation takes on a more significant role than merely contributing to an endeavour. It allows the notion of 'reflection', 'reflective practitioner' (Schön, 1983b), 'teacher as researcher' (Elliott, 1991), and the researcher as tutor to co-exist and provide a dynamic framework for professional development through school-based experiences. The role of the HEI in such an endeavour is pivotal. The Annenburg approach, in the second case study in Chapter 4, shows clearly how HEIs can structure settings that facilitate development by promoting projects to improve classroom practice and student learning through collaborative work environments. These are based on groups of teachers meeting regularly once a month, developing a professional portfolio, participating in peer observations and making a two-year commitment to the project.

Professional education and development in such a setting must allow for and include challenging conceptual structures in order that learning may occur. This applies to all levels of development. Increasingly, professional development should be seen as a vehicle for the enhanced professionalism of teachers, whether this be through mentoring, peer observation, curriculum development, or increased subject knowledge. Partnership must be seen as a joint activity that links the continuum of development. HEIs can stimulate, support and provide settings that allow learning to take place, through questioning and 'constructive criticism'. Such linked activity requires an understanding of what each institution is attempting to do and the reasons for their involvement in the partnership. What is required is to place teachers, teacher educators and researchers within the context of their individual roles and responsibilities.

Day (1995) puts forward an argument relating to the roles and responsibilities of teacher educators and professional development that forms the basis of this discussion. I think it is a very useful starting point. Day focuses upon the 'purposes, prejudices, practices and context of those who teach education in all its forms within higher education and schools'. He suggests that these have been fraught with difficulties and challenges which are founded on historical, social and psychological issues, and as such have to date been reflected in the nature of collaborations that have occurred between schools and HEIs. Although I do not agree with all of Day's assumptions, I am in sympathy with a great many, and particularly with his description of education being purposeful, attentive and rigorous, and which connects with the lives of students and pupils; practice that is reflective and provides opportunity for development and research that is useful and usable (pp.2–3). This in essence forms the basis of a sustained and collaborative framework for partnership. However, all too often research has been separate from professional practice, and increasingly been captured by its own agenda, divergent from the needs and interests of professional practitioners (Rein and White, 1980). The move to school-focused INSET and school-based inquiry should alleviate such problems, and facilitate the development of research for both schools and HEIs. However, Day (1995, p.2) suggests that:

> 'research, then, is a function of every teacher and teacher educator and every teacher and teacher educator can do it – through the "business practice" culture of most schools and initial teacher training sections of many university departments of education. This often initiates against engagement in systematic inquiries, and not all teachers in these contexts are confident or skilled in making these public through writing.'

Where does this leave those in both institutions who wish to develop, whether individually, institutionally or collaboratively? Teachers and teacher educators/researchers do not develop in isolation: they learn from a variety of other people who may have had more experience and are more knowledgeable in specific areas than themselves. In all cases they learn from 'experts' by attending courses or being involved in training on new techniques, whether these be assessment procedures or new statistical approaches to data interpretation.

Hence individuals learn from a variety of sources both inside and outside their institutions. But can existing cultures affect teacher, teacher educator, and researcher development? Hargreaves (1993) suggests that culture carries the community's historically generated and collectively shared solutions to its new and inexperienced membership. It forms a framework for occupational learning (p.217). How does this affect collaboration and partnership? A school-based curriculum development project brings together teachers from a variety of disciplines, all of whom have a common goal: to improve an area of the curriculum they are responsible for. Such a project allows for occupational learning, not just from the individual's point of view, but from a whole-school perspective. Common problems are allowed to surface. A good example can be taken from the first case study in Chapter 4. Three teachers from separate disciplines (science, maths and technology) faced a common problem. Each teacher's department was trying to implement investigative activities into their curriculum, without much success. By joining the group and sharing their concerns, there was a realization that each department was facing similar problems and trying to reinvent the wheel separately. By pooling ideas and working collaboratively, a generic solution was found for investigations across the three subject areas. The final outcome for the school/departments and individual teachers was a greatly improved delivery of investigations with reinforcement of teaching points made by all concerned at strategically timed intervals throughout the year. Pupil achievement was greatly enhanced; this was seen in the end of key stage assessments. This evidence confirms Hargreaves' view that collaborative cultures of teaching help give meaning, support and identity to teachers and their work (ibid., p.217). If this is the case, HEIs can be expected to support inquiry and research that facilitate good practice.

Collaborative environments such as these don't just happen; the role of the HEI is essential in making such conditions operational by supporting initiatives, directing differences and highlighting commonalities. The HEI tutor/researcher also professionally develops, by investigating the ongoing interactions and evaluating the effects they have on collaborative cultures, good practice and learning outcomes. These observations are frequently disseminated in academic journals and conferences. It is, however, this latter element that often mitigates against schools and HEIs collaborating and supporting each other. What has occurred in teacher education to cause this?

Many of the changes in education over the last 20 years have altered the context of teacher education, with many teacher educators having come out of school themselves to enter into a university department of education, where they are obliged to comply with university norms of development, such as research and the publication of research data. To survive has often required compliance, and this naturally has had to take place within the outline of school and teaching. Whether teacher educators felt secure in a research role is not part of the present argument, however; what is important is that research was brought into or performed on teachers and school, thus forming a divide that has led to a participatory relationship. In terms of

professional development this has caused a dilemma for many teacher educators. Do they continue their personal development as good teachers alongside experienced and trainee teachers, or do they pursue research on teaching
and gain academic status?

If professional development is to be a two-way flow between schools and
HEIs then it is essential to accept that for teacher educators both forms of
development need to be recognized by schools and HEIs. To coin a phrase,
'You can't have one without the other'. If schools do not feel a part of teacher
educators' development and as a result do not participate in or facilitate
research, how are teacher educators to research and further develop teacher
education?

What types of contribution are we looking for if schools and HEIs are to
work in partnership? Hargreaves (1995) suggests that:

> 'the specific contribution of university faculties of education to teacher preparation
> should not be based on geographical precedents of where teacher preparation has
> come to be located or historical traditions of what teacher education has done in
> the past. Nor should the university's contribution be based on teacher educators'
> self interested pursuit and protection of their own professionalisation. Rather,
> within the broad partnership of teacher preparation and of teacher education more
> widely, university faculties of education should contribute what they are uniquely
> equipped to do: developing understanding of educational institutes and processes,
> fostering critical reflection about them, and building the skills of inquiry which will
> enable teachers to develop understanding and reflection as a basis, for continuous
> improvement, throughout their professional lives.'

Productive partnerships can only occur if Hargreaves' views are considered
seriously. Both Day and Hargreaves believe that 'without critical intervention
and critical biographical reflection, most teachers fall prey to the influence of
their prior beliefs and assumption' (Bullough, 1991). I would add that such
an idea could equally apply to teacher education, if they are not actively
involved in schools. But this involvement must not be seen as a form of
collaboration that facilitates the need to accumulate evidence for academic
publication. Elliott (1994, p.135) describes this type of relationship as:

> 'collaborative research with teachers not unrelated to the need of academics to
> construct research identities they could live with. It was a road to salvation, to
> romance, to community. The researcher may experience guilt at having dissociated
> her/himself from the "realities" of school teaching in pursuit of a research career.
> Such guilt could be tolerated when thrown in the balance with the quest for the
> grand educational narrative.'

If such scenarios are to be avoided and true partnership developed we must
look for explanations as to why and how continuing professional development can be linked to collaborative teacher research.

Collaboration, although difficult by its very nature of requiring equity
amongst its participants, does offer teachers and teacher educators/researchers

the opportunity to be involved in professional development through systematic investigation of the theory and practice.

Why and How Should CPD be Linked to Education Research?

Professional development is essential to any individuals who wish to further their knowledge and skills, and as such requires a context in which it is to be achieved. As I have previously stated, working relationships and in particular collaborative partnerships need to take account of the existing cultures and contexts within which the partnership operates. This means accepting the differences in the core functions of schools and HEIs. Schools teach pupils, and universities teach adults and pursue research. In effect this can be seen as a constraint on long-term relationships. I would suggest it does not have to be, if the relationship between researcher and researched is equitable (Calhoun and Glickman, 1993; Wahlstrom and King, 1993). What is at the heart of such a relationship is the development of understanding 'difference'. This can best be explained through an example: a school which has low pupil achievement and an identified problem with the teaching of literacy skills. The school wants to raise the standards of literacy throughout the school by introducing new and effective teaching strategies. In order to do this they wish to evaluate their present situation with a view to designing and developing a new literacy programme for the school. The HEI working collaboratively on this project could support the development by creating an environment whereby the school can investigate the issues and problems related to literacy in a systematic and analytical way, through coordinated planning and timing of tasks that would provide the necessary evidence on which to design and develop any future programme. Running parallel to the school improvement project the HEI may be researching literacy programmes and their effectiveness in a wider context. If this is the case each party's needs should be clearly stated and both the researched and the researcher have equitable status in the project. In order to develop knowledge, teachers and researchers have to establish and explain the boundaries within which they are operating. In a collaborative partnership this means the context in which teaching, learning, and research occurs.

Increasingly there is an assumption that teachers' continued professional development should be linked to educational research. How should this assumption be perceived? The link can be seen as one that gives independence to teachers through theoretical and practical means, which can be supported by schools and HEIs as a way to increasing personal knowledge and methods by which this knowledge can be made applicable to the classroom situation. This clearly is the case of the school enquiring into literacy. Accepting that there is a difference between types of research that can take place in schools can create tensions, but these should be openly discussed when developing partnership roles across schools and HEIs. Day (1993b, p.13) suggests that:

> 'the recognition of a need to develop a new language for communication between teachers and academics (Nias, 1991); and the establishment of self-critical, self-reflecting communities (Handal, 1991), whilst attractive, depend for their fulfilment upon the willingness, social skills and abilities of participants to create and negotiate contracts, either collectively or individually, which is based on forms of critical friendship.'

The implication of this statement is that professional development through educational research presents teachers and teacher educators with an opportunity of widening their horizons and constructing meaning for themselves beyond the classroom. This view of professional development not only *requires* partnership but *depends* upon it. Working in such a relationship necessitates all participants to have a 'voice'. The nature of voice can be identified in a variety of ways, from debriefing in peer observation to improve practice, to identifying common areas for discussion and enquiry in subject-based curriculum development. In this way failures and uncertainty are not protected and defended, but shared and discussed with a view to gaining help and support (Nias, 1989). It allows the focus of the collaboration to be on the person for whom the development is intended.

Researching into education should be viewed as a challenge within a sustained environment as a means of promoting not only individual professional development, but also furthering the development of education. However, it is also important that in the future, teachers' perspectives are recognized in the initiation of research, development and evaluation, and through contracted, negotiated partnerships, and in any accounts and reports that may result (Day, 1995). Teachers should be encouraged to contribute to research articles as a way of increasing their own professionalism.

The political changes discussed at the beginning of this chapter have initiated and encouraged HEIs and schools working together through partnership in the training of teachers. Parallel to this has been the emergence of LMS which has given a centrality to teacher management. As a consequence, schools and HEIs have looked to alternative forms of teacher development. Increasingly schools have looked for courses and projects that are of direct relevance to the school, its management and learning outcomes. HEIs have tried to respond in a variety of ways, including school-based research projects, long- and short-term award-bearing courses, as well as specific curriculum inputs.

Each institution has had its own agendas for either looking for or creating avenues for development. More recently it is being recognized that each institution requires the other, and that choice is an important factor when considering and constructing a partnership agreement. Choice does offer institutions the opportunity to develop new and creative ways of collaborating. Within the HEI framework, teachers may come into the HEI and lecture trainee teachers, while the tutor teaches in school, thus keeping their own development recent in the classroom context. At the same time the classroom teacher has the opportunity of trying out a variety of alternative teaching techniques with trainee teachers. Collaboration of this type is proving very successful in the ITE sector. Equally successful in the field of school-based curriculum development is teachers adopting a role of associate tutor and providing the link between school and the HEI. The pressures of choice and change in the market economy are considerable for schools and HEIs. Both are required to adapt to an ever more competitive market forced on them by external agencies. It would therefore seem reasonable and logical that collaborative partnerships should accord a much greater say in the *what* and the *how* of specific provision and the methods chosen to address the issues.

The introduction of school-based ITE and INSET has allowed schools to identify and provide the focus for ITE and INSET activities, and where these activities should take place. Perry's (1977) definition of INSET suggests that the needs of both school and individual teachers will be considered. This has led to schools negotiating with a variety of agencies to provide for those needs. Partnership has been one way of addressing this issue, by providing award-bearing courses that have been aligned to school-based work that brings joint benefits:

- the recognition of individual teacher development;
- validation of school-based research and development as an aspect of professionalism;
- curriculum development for the school, leading to increased learning outcomes.

Schools and award-giving institutions should collaborate more fully and frequently in the ways that have been described. These examples provide institutions with creative and dynamic opportunities for development.

Chapter 3

The Need to Collaborate

If a collaborative partnership is to be entered into and to succeed institutions require an understanding of what is to be undertaken. This chapter aims to facilitate such an understanding by stimulating discussion through examples. It focuses on three key areas related to collaboration:

1. Why do schools and HEIs need to collaborate?
2. What should the nature of collaboration be?
3. What are the likely pitfalls in a collaborative approach?

I put forward a practical framework from which institutions can develop a collaborative partnership. Particular attention is given to the steps to be considered prior to entering a collaborative initiative.

The final aspect of the chapter draws on work by Fullan and Hargreaves relating to institutional cultures, and how these may affect the way individuals act and react within institutional contexts. Each of these elements show how professional development can be thought of, and the types of activities that teachers may engage in through a collaborative partnership, in order to facilitate such development.

Why do Schools and HEIs Need to Collaborate?

In essence it would seem the common sense thing to do, but there are many other reasons why collaboration should take place. The changes that have taken place within education both at school and HEI in terms of ITE and CPD have forced institutions to consider working jointly. Such ventures have always taken place, but following Circular 9/92 (DfE, 1992) these relationships have had to be formalized. Added to this, school-focused INSET required HEIs to rethink what their roles were in the context of delivering professional development work to teachers.

Professional development in the 1990s is no longer a privately pursued optional extra, but a publicly implied, accountable part of every teacher's regular working life (Day, 1993b, p.87). For this to happen we need to break away from traditional roles and relationships. Teachers are entitled to, and require support for, their development, both personal and in areas of improvement required by their institutions. Placing such development in context requires institutions to have a clear understanding of their development needs as well as those of individuals within the institution. An over-riding issue is to establish where and how those needs are to be addressed and met so that the school can achieve its overall aims of improvement.

Collaborative partnership is the way forward. It requires shared leadership and methodological value if it is to succeed. For this to happen schools and HEIs need each other. If schools are to improve and school-based research is one aspect by which they can, HEIs have a significant role to play in supporting such improvement. They have the ability to be an impartial 'critical friend', by directing and ensuring that the methodologies of enquiry are both sound and of quality. Collaboration of this nature should be seen as not only affecting teachers, but teacher educators and researchers. This brings me back to a quote from Lieberman I used earlier in the book; her challenge was to 'create a community that educates all of us, those in the university and those in the school, a community that expands our relationships with one another, and in so doing, our knowledge and our effectiveness' (1992, p.12).

In order to become more effective there needs to be an understanding of the process that creates improvement. This type of process is exemplified in a school that identifies low achievement in specific departments. Quite rightly they would wish to raise the standards within them. How and in what way? The school and the HEI approach the problem together, establishing areas of weakness and strengths within the school as a means of identifying why there is a problem in specific departments, and the nature of the perceived problems. A plan of action is then drawn up targeting the areas of weakness. The HEI can support such action in a variety of ways, including whole-school directed INSET, working alongside individual departments or individual teachers. Working in this way requires trust, confidence and the ability to understand that the process of collaborative partnership is supportive and non-threatening. It is one that is aimed at increasing all participants' knowledge of achievement, and how this knowledge can be used holistically within a whole-school improvement programme. The HEI's role is crucial, as it is supportive and non-judgmental, unlike inspections. HMIs and OFSTED come into institutions and often indicate what is wrong, but make no suggestions on how to improve. Collaborative partnership allows schools and HEIs to identify areas of concern, build pragmatic and workable solutions to the identified areas and evaluate successes and failures together. HEIs can support and give constructive criticism to help the process of improvement forward.

Collaborative partnerships provide a pathway for mutual professional development and change for both institutions. But why do institutions need this type of change? Because increasingly the concept and responsibilities associated with professional development need to be shared, success depends upon the social, psychological and cultural contexts of institutions being understood. What better way for HEIs to understand the problems associated with school improvement than to be directly involved in that improvement process? Equally schools working in collaboration with HEIs begin to understand the process required to identify issues such as low achievement, low pupil expectations, differing teaching styles and learning outcomes, as well as the methods needed to take such problems forward and improve progressively and effectively. Fullan (1993) expresses this eloquently and reinforces my argument by suggesting that:

> 'Teacher development and institutional development [of universities and schools] must go hand in hand. You can't have one without the other. If there was ever a symbiotic relationship that makes complete sense it is the collaboration of universities and school systems in the initial and on going development of educators. The cultures of course differ.... But they do and are increasingly coming together to create more powerful, and sustained learning communities for student teachers, beginning teachers, experienced teachers and university professors. This is one case where synergy can be achieved.' (p.121)

Fullan states that reform in teacher education must begin simultaneously in schools and in faculties of education, both independently and together through alliance (ibid., p.121)

This is essentially true of our present situation in England. School-based ITE has forced partnership on institutions, and the introduction of school-based teacher-research funded by the TTA has made HEIs reconsider their position in such research. Within this context I suggest five reasons why schools and HEIs need collaborative partnership:

1. To have a shared understanding of what educational research should be and for what purpose it will be conducted and disseminated.
2. To plan and innovate teacher development initiatives that support school improvement and the knowledge required to understand school improvement.
3. To plan and develop initial teacher education initiatives that enhance the quality of teaching and learning and the knowledge required to construct new meanings of effective teaching and learning.
4. To increase individual teachers', teacher educators' and researchers' personal and process knowledge.
5. To develop strategies for disseminating collaborative findings as a means of enhancing professional development across the educational forums.

These reasons are broad but encompass all areas currently under debate in

England and Wales. The five statements highlight the need to consider what development is and where it should be going. It is clear that in the future professional development and institutional improvement will need to recognize responsibility through collaborative partnership. Day (1993a) sums up my argument by stating that:

> 'Unless we focus more upon the building of structural networks not only between individuals within institutions but between institutions themselves, then much reflection for learning may remain at the private "practical" level.' (p.30)

When collaborative partnership exists school improvement issues are shared. Increasingly schools have to meet post-OFSTED recommendations in order to make themselves more effective. This requires considerable planning by school staff development managers, in terms of the INSET provision needed to meet both short- and long-term development of individual teachers and departments. Working in conjunction with HEIs a systematic programme that includes accreditation can be formulated, implemented and evaluated with respect to the targets set. Joint planning and monitoring is of benefit to both institutions. Working in this way increases schools' choice and allows them to be, in Giddens' (1995) terms, 'reflective about their choices'.

Schools and HEIs need each other to succeed. Strong partnerships will not happen by accident, good will or establishing ad hoc projects. They require new structures, new activities, and a rethinking of the internal workings of each institution as well as their inter-institutional workings (Watson and Fullan, 1992, p.219). A clear example is the role of the link tutor in school-based ITE courses. The link tutor collaborates with schools and HEI in meeting the needs of mentors and student teachers, despite their roles being perceived differently by the respective institutions.

Ultimately growth and development of any partnership will occur when connections are made between the differences in institutions rather than the similarities; as Dewey (1934) suggests, it is dependent upon the positive appreciation of difference. Schools and HEIs are dissimilar in key aspects of structure, culture and reward systems, and that is why they need each other to collaborate and take professional development into the next millennium. Working together can potentially provide the coherence, coordination and development that is presently lacking and so desperately needed. Understanding the processes of school improvement and the individual's role within that process is fundamental to success.

What Should the Nature of Collaboration Be?

Throughout the text I have, like many others before me, suggested that professional development is one of the most promising and powerful routes to both individual and institutional development. It seems a common sense thing to do, and research continually shows that teachers and teacher educators have faith in its potential. If such faith prevails, what is or should be the nature of such development? Loucks-Horsley *et al.* (1987, p.7) state that:

> 'Teacher development is a complex process whose success depends upon a favourable context for learning and practical, engaging activities. Availability of resources, flexible working conditions, support and recognition can make all the difference in the desire of teachers to refine their practice. Similarly, staff development experiences that build on collegiality, collaboration, discovery and solving real problems of teaching and learning summon the strength within a staff, instead of just challenging them to measure up to somebody else's standard. The focal point for staff development is the individual, working with others.... When staff development emphasises an idea or approach without considering the person(s) who will implement it, the design and results are weakened.'

There is no doubt that the notion of teacher development is complex and challenging, requiring a variety of skills and knowledge. What is clear is that successful development is both a strategy for 'specific, instructional change and a strategy for basic organisational change in the way teachers [teacher educators] work and learn together' (Fullan, 1990).

Collaboration (and specifically collaborative partnership) is a way of addressing the above. A framework for collaboration gives insight into the types of function that can be performed: facilitating, supporting, informing and prescribing (Johnson *et al.*, 1996), as well as recognizing and acknowledging that teachers are knowledge generators (Lytle and Cochran-Smith, 1992).

Teachers and teacher educators/researchers have the opportunity to collaborate within ITE and school-based INSET projects, allowing them to form a synthesis of what each knows and considers important about the teaching/learning process. Collaborative partnership aims to build a community of collaborative learners focused on inquiry and knowledge production as a form of continual professional development. The nature of development that occurs through mentor discussions with both students and HEI tutors is fundamental to improving the quality of teaching and learning in schools, as well as providing an avenue to understand the processes involved in this type of development. In order to improve learning situations it is necessary to become involved in ideas and matters outside the immediate setting (Fullan, 1993, p.83). What better way to achieve such aims than through a partnership that has purpose and a clear understanding of what the nature of the collaboration should be? I have identified ten elements essential to collaborative change, grouped into four main categories:

- *Shared leadership* which requires:
  - the belief that working together is valued by both institutions;
  - working together to be seen as a scheduled activity giving status to what is being developed; however, it must not stifle the individual's own development;

- the participating individuals to share in a great deal of the work and effort that is needed to craft an effective and sustained collaboration.

- *Sharing of the learning process* which requires:
  - an evolving process that allows a knowledge base to be created with respect to school effectiveness, institutional development and a collaborative framework;
  - an understanding of what it is to work in genuine collaboration.

- *Establishing trust and equity* which requires:
  - mutual trust and respect, reflecting equity among participants;
  - an open appreciation of the needs of those involved; there must be no hidden agenda to the collaboration;
  - developing skills and initiatives that allow for change and development to be supported.

- *Respecting cultural and contextual differences* which requires:
  - understanding that school and HEI cultures differ and that their difference focuses on similar issues such as reward systems;
  - understanding that context will play a crucial factor in developing a collaborative partnership.

The context of the partnership has to be based on a pragmatic collaborative framework. I do not wish to give the impression that this is either easy or obtainable, but it is an objective worth working towards.

Shared leadership

Collaboration allows for the sharing of problems and pressures. In our present climate of continual change collaboration should allow schools and HEIs to shoulder these changes together, not in isolation, but in partnership. Circulars 9/92 (DfE, 1992) and 14/93 (DfE, 1993a) clearly indicated that partnership is essential to the future of teacher education and long-term professional development initiatives. The implication of this is that increasingly schools and HEIs have to share responsibility for such developments, which demands shared leadership. But what does shared leadership mean and how can it be implemented?

If collaborative partnership is to evolve, the concept of leadership needs to be considered, understood and applied to the context of the anticipated relationship.

'Leadership involves empowerment, and as such necessitates a shared responsibility. The partnership ethic must be encultured at all individual levels and organisational levels.... The more leadership is spread around, the better off the partnership will be.... Power, however, is not a finite concept. The more it is shared, the more there seems to be. And with power comes responsibility; responsible

leadership entails creating the opportunities for responsible leadership in others.'
(Goodlad, 1993, p.33)

School-based ITE schemes offer the type of opportunity Goodlad describes. ITE has many areas of responsibility both in schools and HEIs. Sharing these does not mean everybody has to do the same tasks; it means taking responsibility for those areas that each contributor to the scheme does best. This can only happen if there is shared and responsible leadership.

Empowerment and leadership can make or break any partnership development. In fact, it is a prime area for possible conflict and struggle. This is particularly pertinent when establishing aims, objectives, goals and priorities within a school-HEI relationship.

> 'It is critical that the partnership process model of collaboration in substantive, tangible ways is: An ethic of collaboration and collaborative inquiry and action, more than anything else, characterises the processes that go on in a school–university partnership. What it means to collaborate needs to be modelled every step of the way. Since building partnerships is mostly a two-steps-forward/one-step-backward kind of activity, inappropriate, unilateral decisions can destroy process.'
> (Sirotnik, 1988, cited in Goodlad, 1993, p.31)

This clearly indicates that dialogue through negotiated meaning creates a successful sharing of power between schools and HEIs. Such understanding clearly comes through in the case studies cited in Chapter 4. Their relative successes and failures lay in the understanding or misunderstanding of leadership of the initiatives. Successful leadership allows the re-specification of aims and objectives by enabling equity and teachers being given the freedom to develop and be acknowledged as knowledge generators. Increasingly professional tutors or mentors in schools are devising alternative strategies for teaching and developing initial teacher trainees. This knowledge generation is shared with HEIs and partnership is taken forward in a mature way. The sharing of responsibility and leadership is equitable and leads to personal and institutional development. It is imperative that both teachers and teacher educators/researchers assume leadership roles within the collaborative partnership. HEI tutors need to be actively involved in teaching 'real pupils' and teachers need to examine more theoretical perspectives that may underpin a change in their practice. This will facilitate a dynamic two-way flow of knowledge and expertise.

It is an important challenge for institutional improvement. It means teachers and teacher educators have to reconstruct the principles of collaboration within the context of making schools and courses effective. This requires both parties to articulate, listen and bring together different voices in the educational and social community, and to establish guiding principles around which these voices and their purposes can cohere (Hargreaves, 1995, p.170).

Nowhere is this more crucial than in school-HEI partnerships. Teachers, teacher educators and researchers are all equally able to draw on a wide range of intellectual and social skills, knowledge bases, perceptions and attitudes. A partnership needs this to be acknowledged. Research by Bickel and Hattrup (1995) shows that teachers have the capacity to bring applied classroom instructional knowledge that helps the understanding initiated by research. Raising achievement in a maths class may seem an impossible task to a teacher working in isolation, but to a supportive observer of that class the task may seem not quite so problematic.

The teacher and observer can meet to discuss the problems. The teacher can bring a wealth of instructional knowledge and craft skills to the discussion and, when put into the context of the observations, can change the teaching strategies employed, therefore increasing pupils' learning potential and outcomes and raising their overall achievement. The teacher's voice within such situations has to be valued for the contribution it can and does make to changing practice. It involves considering the teacher as a professional. This is a positive aspect of collaborative change in the context of research and development. Direct observation of classroom practice initiates discussion and reflection on what has taken place. It necessitates a shared vision of professionalism, one that nurtures self-reflection, increasing one's knowledge base about teaching and learning, and contributes to this knowledge base by sharing research findings in a user-friendly and pragmatic way. This approach is exemplified in the Annenburg model of development, discussed in Chapter 4.

Professional development must be perceived as a continuum and an ongoing process, with leadership being part of that continuum, and one which teachers and teacher educators must experience. In a traditional view of leadership there is a basic assumption that 'people are powerless, their lack of personal vision, and inability to master the forces of change, deficits which can be remedied only by a few great leaders' (Senge, 1990, p.340). This view is no longer applicable to today's schools and HEIs. What is required is leadership that allows institutions to develop and grow, giving the individuals within the institution opportunities to increase their knowledge and capabilities, to understand complex issues, discuss their visions and the way forward. Senge (1990) sees three key areas of importance within this 'new leadership': leader as designer, as steward, and as teacher. It is possible through dialogue in a shared leadership between institutions to allow these three areas to develop. Fullan and Hargreaves (1991) give excellent practical advice that would help develop shared leadership:

1. understand the culture of the school (HEI);
2. value your teachers (teacher educators/researchers): promote their professional growth;
3. extend what is valued;

4. express what is valued;
5. promote collaboration, not cooperation;
6. make menus, not mandates;
7. use bureaucratic means to facilitate, not constrain;
8. connect with the wider environment and educational community.
   (Adapted from Fullan and Hargreaves, 1991, p.112)

Schools and HEIs have many opportunities for shared leadership. Teachers are frequently given leadership roles within the new ITE schemes: as mentors, or professional tutors, or in school-based INSET initiatives they become the site-based or consortium-based coordinators. They allow those in a new leadership role to develop an understanding of the dynamic and complex processes of change (Fullan, 1993).

Shared leadership involves empowerment, and if this empowerment is to be constructive, and enhance the quality of partnership and the development of those involved, certain practical steps need to be taken. Stacey (1992) offers seven steps to leadership. I have used these as a framework and adapted them to suit what I think shared leadership within a collaborative partnership should embody:

1. Developing a joint understanding of systems and control mechanisms.
2. Designing and developing joint users of appropriate power.
3. Establishing and nurturing self-organizing learning teams.
4. Developing an appreciation for multiple contexts and cultures.
5. Developing mutuality in order to take joint risks.
6. Designing and developing joint strategies to improve group learning skills.
7. Pooling and creating joint resources.
   (Adapted from Stacey, 1992, p.188)

These elements need to be developed and based on the essential features of trust and equity. I would like to use an analogy here, by comparing collaborative partnership to making a quality cake. If the ingredients used to make the cake are top quality, the end product is more likely to be of excellent quality, provided a suitable method for making the cake is chosen. The same applies to shared leadership: the ingredients may be there, but if inappropriate methods are used, a poor quality product will be the outcome.

Sharing the learning process

Understanding the meaning-making process (Fullan and Stieglbauer, 1991) when interactions occur both between individuals and institutions requires a synthesis of what each community knows about the process. It certainly is an evolving process, and must allow the participants to create a knowledge base from which to operate and develop. Schools need to know how HEIs select students for ITE courses; they need to know the rationale behind INSET courses or Masters level courses. Similarly HEIs need to know why and how schools choose departments and mentors for ITE placements. Understanding these contextual differences is essential to collaborative success.

What characterizes interactions between institutions and individuals is more to do with learning than teaching. It is usually a different kind of experience than that of attending a taught course, seminar or a specific INSET session delivered by a consultant or internal 'expert'. Yet peer interactions can be organized to have a 'tutorial' type quality, whereby a peer can be assigned to lead, by taking a 'tutor' role. Such a role is educationally valuable because the 'tutors' themselves may learn from the experience. For example, teacher educators may teach a class that is being researched by the novice teacher to gain a true understanding of the problems associated with teaching a specific class, or teachers may lead a discussion on the types of questions that need to be raised in order to inquire into improved learning outcomes. This type of sharing is one approach to schools and HEIs learning from each other. Peer observation of this nature requires sensitivity and trust, which takes considerable time to evolve and secure.

An alternative is cooperative learning. This relates to the strategies for managing tasks that often implicate the whole group or institutions that are working together. Here learning takes place through the proportioning of tasks within the partnership, so that individuals take on differing responsibilities. This is demonstrated in the Annenburg model and the school-based curriculum development project described in Chapter 4. If such a strategy is to work, considerable organizational skills are required to sustain motivation, continued learning and development. Frequently motivation is enhanced through reward systems and, as already stated, these are different for schools and HEIs. Therefore each must understand and state their intentions within the partnership, otherwise it is doomed to failure.

Shared learning and collaborative groups are underpinned by the psychological context – the cognitive processes that individuals engage in. What is important here is to make a clear distinction between cooperative and collaborative learning that would facilitate professional development.

Cooperative learning helps to define a motivational and organizational structure for a collaborative partnership; while collaborative learning focuses on the cognitive advantages that arise within the more intimate exchanges of working together (Slavin, 1987). For shared learning to occur, a closer look at the type and detail of the interactions that such partnership activities afford is necessary. This allows identification of the distinctive strengths and weaknesses of such interactions. By concentrating on strengths and weaknesses, a number of processes that influence the social contexts of the interactions emerge. I believe that there are three that underpin shared learning. Much of my thinking here has been influenced by the research of Johnson and Johnson (1985):

- Communication and articulation.
- Conflict and difference (both internal and external).
- Shared construction and meaning.

Communication and articulation

Communication and articulation are essential if ideas are to be explored. They provide a way for individuals to gain understanding by being required to make their thinking explicit and public. Collaborative partnership within ITE enables this to happen. Bringing subject mentors together for one-day conferences to discuss subject-based issues is crucial to teacher development at all levels. By communicating ideas, the knowledge base from which teachers and teacher educators operate is increased and discussion of common problems is encouraged. Similar parallels can be drawn with collaborative school-based INSET projects. Teachers can articulate their ideas and discuss differences through a variety of means. For example, maths and PE teachers can discuss gifted children. What makes these pupils gifted? How can they be helped to progress? HEIs can support such interactions and motivate teachers to ask the types of questions that are all too often left unasked. The articulation of opinions, hypotheses or interpretations of events, benefits any joint activity that may take place, by enabling individuals to self-reflect. Public articulation reflects the more interactive (rather than declarative) quality of learning.

Conflict and difference

The nature of disagreement between individuals or institutions can be thought of as a way of resolving problems. The convention of conversation is that disagreement should prompt discursive moves of justification and negotiation. It therefore can be considered as a positive and productive way to promote learning. Conflict is a cognitive element associated with Piaget, and draws attention to the power of argument, or 'the shock of our thoughts coming into contact with that of others' (Piaget, 1928, p.204). Taking this point further, it would suggest that individuals from schools and HEIs can benefit from encountering differences (during argument), as a way of enforcing reflection and rethinking perspectives. Undoubtedly such rethinking and further discussion can only facilitate genuine collaboration.

Shared construction and meaning

Shared construction and meaning is influenced by, and arises from, Vygotsky's socio-cultural thinking. It allows individuals to take responsibility for complementary tasks while trying to solve a problem such as the gifted child in differing subject areas. This is often organized in discussion about the overall context of the problem. It is a way of seeing problems and ways forward as a joint activity, where creativity is dispersed and strategies of sharing responsibilities serve to accelerate the participants' development.

Socially constructed meaning allows the individual to share and learn through joint activity, but develop individually. Schools and HEIs are in a position to consider and adopt approaches to collaborative partnership which incorporate these notions of continual professional development.

Establishing trust and equity

Taking responsibility for school improvement that includes CPD and educational change through collaborative partnerships does not involve a process whereby one institution prescribes and the other enacts. Collaboration involves institutions and the people within them having mutual trust and respect, seeing themselves as critical friends, understanding and appreciating their differing needs and genuinely caring for each other's development.

Developing skills and initiatives that allow for change requires collaborations to be supportive, not ones that view interventions as imposed by outsiders. They need to evolve allowing for reflection on practice and perceptions as well as procedures and goals. These ideals can only be achieved through equity and shared leadership. Thinking in these terms would take schools and HEIs nearer to the concept of continual professional development being a continuum from the beginning teacher to the university professor.

Respecting cultural and contextual differences

In concluding their research on collaboration, Bickel and Hattrup (1995, p.53) suggest that:

> 'differences in institutional cultures are bound to produce conflict in sustained, substantive collaborations. Just as individual teachers and researchers bring to a collaboration differing experiences, values and incentive systems for participants, so do the collaborating institutions. As with individuals, such differences are an important factor that will influence the direction of the collaboration.'

Within the English school-based curriculum development project such differences surfaced in the context of teacher needs and pressures and HEIs' need to meet submission deadlines. Neither was not always supportive of the other, but sustained dialogue over a period of time improved this situation by introducing two submission dates within the year, hence giving teachers more flexibility and reducing the pressure of possible failure. This example highlights and reaffirms Bickel's findings that successful institutional collaborations can be built around the meeting of self- or mutual institutional interests, or some of both (ibid., p.54).

Crossing the cultural divide requires a shared language in order for professional relationships to develop. Although schools and HEIs are all involved in the process of education they belong to 'different discourse communities' (Gee, 1990), which hold different values and are set within different contexts. These contexts determine the way each approaches and conducts their work, and are often neither appreciated nor acknowledged by individuals or institutions.

Let us consider some classic examples. Schools might identify an area of concern, or a problem that requires resolving through INSET or consultative work through an HEI. The notion of a 'problem' or 'area of concern' is frequently defined, implicitly, by the HEI participant as a possibly interesting area for research. However, the 'problems' or 'areas of concern' are divisive concepts. For teachers problems often mean a fault in their practice; for schools, problems are often thought of as areas that require improvement. This appears to give the impression that HEIs are casting doubts on teachers' and schools' abilities to manage their 'problems'. Yet for the researcher, 'problem' means something to be analysed in a way that will produce a deeper understanding of the inherent situation.

Miller (1990) reinforces my argument when discussing the words and terms teacher educators/researchers, as opposed to teachers, use when considering practice and school improvement. Teacher educators frequently use terms that are considered educationally significant, such as 'empowerment', 'emancipation' and 'professionalism'. Yet as Miller points out:

> 'These words were not the ones that teachers most often used to describe the conditions and situations in which they wished to teach. Most often, it seemed to me, teachers spoke of caring about kids, of wanting to help them in their struggle to grow and learn.... These were personal words, the words of teachers who worked in daily situations in which the notions as well as the language of "empowerment" and "emancipation" seemed distant, even foreign to their lives.' (p.16)

Appreciating and acknowledging such cultural and contextual differences have a significant effect on the outcomes of collaborative partnerships and eventual educational changes. Schools and HEIs need to look for common meaning when establishing projects leading to school improvement. When is a problem a research question or an area of enquiry to be explored in a collaborative and supportive way? Understanding of these context-bound issues must be on schools' and HEIs' agendas when discussing collaborative projects. Each step towards collaboration is difficult, but it must be placed within a context of mutual investment and the search for improved education through continuing professional development. However dedicated one is to collaboration, pitfalls are inevitable but avoidable.

What are the likely Pitfalls in Collaboration?

A major element in successful collaboration is the understanding that new roles and responsibilities are required. Breaking away from traditional leader and follower roles is vital to collaborative partnership. Equity and a shared power base are essential ingredients, requiring dialogue and often incurring tension and conflict, but as Lieberman (1989, p.36) suggests:

> 'Working in bureaucratic settings has taught everyone to be compliant, to be rule governed, not to ask questions, seek alternatives or deal with competing values. People are supposed to follow orders from those at the top. Working to create more professional cultures in schools, however, calls upon people to engage in discussion to seek a collective vision and the practical means to achieve it. Instead of one leader and many followers, a leader... works to facilitate leadership and encourage it among entire staff.... Developers, like others in the educational establishment, must define their success not by becoming yet another group of specialists, but rather by engaging in the building of a culture of inquiry and improved learning environments.'

A view that is often put forward by teacher educators/researchers when they enter into a collaborative partnership is that of empowering teachers by facilitating their involvement in research concerning their pupils' learning and their own practice. This is both a limited and naive view of collaborative partnership. Collaboration and successful professional development within the context described by Lieberman necessitates a system that enables all participants within the collaboration to be actively involved in decision-making and to share what they feel is of value. In fact, teachers and teacher educators require time to think critically about what the term 'collaboration' means, by considering how others have come to define it, and as a result construct a joint vision of what collaboration should be and the role they perceive they have within the project. Setting ground rules is difficult but a prerequisite to success. If a collaborative partnership is viewed as something that only affects the teacher or merely serves to facilitate the researcher then it will be doomed to failure. It must be seen as something that can change and benefit all within the partnership.

A definition of a sustainable partnership is provided by Tikunoff et al. (1979) who perceive it to be as 'teacher, researcher, trainer and developer working with parity and assuming equal responsibility to identify, inquire into and resolve the problems and concerns of the classroom teacher' (p.10). I would add to this, 'and conceptualize issues of classroom practice for teacher educators'.

I have suggested that joint ownership is a good and necessary requirement of the collaborative approach. However, we cannot escape the fact that joint ownership is not always seen as the most effective way of empowering all involved. Participants may not wish to give the same amount of time, energy and commitment. It is an issue that can have negative effects on the partnership. This can be overcome if participants are made to feel they have something to contribute and that they bring with them their own expertise. If they see collaboration as a means of achieving pre-specified aims through working together in ways that are of mutual benefit, the endeavour will have a greater chance of success.

One of the major pitfalls in collaboration between institutions is the lack of 'collaborative cultures'. Such cultures require understanding of the immediate contexts in which teachers and teacher educators operate. Educational cultures include the relationship between teachers and their colleagues, teacher educators/researchers and their colleagues, and are among the most educationally significant aspects of teachers' lives and work. They provide a vital context for teacher development (Hargreaves, 1993, p.217).

Culture is an influential element in inter-institutional collaboration as it carries the community's historically generated and collectively shared solutions. As I have argued previously these are considerably different for schools and HEIs. Hargreaves suggests that in order to understand teacher culture, and I would add HEI culture, requires many of the limits to and possibilities of teacher development and educational change to be understood (ibid., p.220).

The significant pitfall to collaborative partnership is that teacher culture is often recognized but not acknowledged when attempting to develop the partnership. Such partnership ignores what Habermas (1971) calls 'communicative rationality', which is concerned with the way in which people in interaction are involved in reaching an understanding. Any partnership must take account of the fact that any action must be based on the achievement of shared understanding. Habermas' argument can be taken one stage further when considering the implications of interactions and sustained collaboration. It is essential that those involved understand that when people come together in encounters, or joint action, they are primarily engaged in achieving some understanding as a basis for further interaction to occur. Language plays a vital role in this context, and as Bruner (1989) argues, language is culture bound. Therefore, it is imperative that when partnership is contemplated, the language of school culture and the language of HEIs are understood and acknowledged within the context of the envisaged working relationship, so that all participants are free to have their say and have equal chances to express their views. Language is effectively the way forward in achieving meaning and collaboration. This in turn will create the basis of a shared understanding such that each party may discuss their anxieties and aspirations, and the resulting action is motivated through discourse and reason.

Collaborative partnerships that ignore culture, context and communicative action will not meet the fundamentals of developing individuals' knowledge and process skills, nor will it improve practice. If institutions choose to ignore such important issues when considering partnership, it will lead to what Hargreaves (1993, p.228) calls 'bounded collaboration'. This is a form of collaboration which does not reach deep down to the grounds, the principles or the ethics of practice, but which stays routine, advice-giving, trick-trading and material-sharing. It is a collaboration which focuses on the immediate and the practical to the exclusion of long-term planning concerns (pp.228–9). Giving ITE placements with no view to training mentors or being committed to the development of teachers, negates collaborative partnership. Well-planned ITE in schools acts as a catalyst for long-term teacher development and school improvement. The same can be said of one-day INSET sessions aimed at changing teaching/learning styles in a school. Single inputs of this nature are both ineffectual and unrealistic in terms of long-term development. Changing teaching/learning styles requires long-term support which HEIs can and should offer.

Collaborative partnerships will not happen overnight, they will evolve slowly. For this reason they may appear unattractive, cumbersome and possibly ineffectual to institutions that are looking for swift 'change' and implementation, whether in response to OFSTED recommendations or research assessment exercise demands. However, it is well established that it is the short sharp change and implementation that fails, as it addresses the immediate but not the long-term problem of development and improvement.

Collaborative partnership falls down on a lack of understanding and acknowledgement of the cultural and contextual differences between schools and HEIs. Hargreaves (1995) suggests that the interpretations given to context help us to understand what factors shape patterns of teaching and teacher development; I would suggest the same applies to HEIs. But there is a need to move beyond this, a need to explore and understand what Hargreaves calls the 'how and why' factors of interaction (ibid., p.156). Only then will collaborative partnerships emerge as a way forward for teacher and teacher educator/researcher development, and institutional improvement. These factors point to an important shift in the context of teaching and researching in education.

In conclusion, a culture that promotes collaboration, trust, mutuality, equity, the taking of risks and a focus on continuous learning and development of pupils and adults, is a key feature for any institutional improvement.

Lessons about Collaboration

In concluding this chapter, I wish to focus on some of the lessons learnt through examining the potential of collaborative partnership and the implications they may have for the future. These are best discussed as a series of statements. For successful collaboration to occur:

- Teachers and teacher educators/researchers have to be *willing* to reconceptualize their roles, their work, and the way they work together.
- Schools and HEIs need to increase their understanding of each other's cultures and the contexts in which they operate, through shared dialogue, as opposed to shared work.
- Everyone does not have to do everything, but participants gain from the interaction in which they are involved.
- Dialogue should be used as a means of achieving parity and equity, but at the same time must allow all participants the opportunity of mutual reflection, development, growth and change.
- Schools and HEIs need to appreciate and acknowledge the 'differences' between them in terms of their needs, both by individuals and institutions.
- A common language needs to be constructed so that thoughts, ideas, vision and anxieties can be communicated without damaging the partnership.
- There needs to be a recognition of the dynamics of status and power inherent in those involved within the partnership, both institutional and individual.
- An appreciation and understanding of the nature of questions being asked are necessary to promote professional development; in other words, who is asking the question and to whom they are important.
- A shared leadership based on trust and equity needs to be established.
- There needs to be an understanding of what information is to be gathered, used, reported or documented and for whom it is intended.

These are some of the basic lessons learnt through both the NSRFP project in the USA and the Ashford project in England, which are discussed in the next chapter. They are by no means definitive, and as my colleagues in the States and in England continue to explore the boundaries of collaborative enterprises, the statements will undoubtedly be challenged, changed and refined. They do, however, give a concrete start for any who wish to enter such a partnership. Dialogue and communication are the essence of success and I finish this chapter with a quote from Clark (1991, p.3) which encapsulates what a collaborative partnership should be. It is:

> 'a stance that transforms communicating people into coequal collaborators who cooperate in the process of negotiating meanings they can truly share, meanings that do not embody the dominance of one [but] enable people to develop a shared understanding of their common experience in an interaction that becomes more than the sum of its individual participants because the shared knowledge that emerges from it cannot be reduced to what each one of them separately knows.'

Chapter 4

Case Studies:
Successes and Failures

Introduction

CPD schools (Fullan, 1994) and school-based INSET have been the centre of discussion within the school improvement movement. Throughout these dialogues collaboration, cooperation and partnership have been stressed, with a variety of models and philosophical standpoints put forward. An equal variety of methods to facilitate the models has been recorded.

Within this chapter two differing models of professional development are considered, one in the USA based at a Southern Californian High School, following the Annenberg model of continuing professional development, and one in the UK following a school-based curriculum development project.

The place of collaborative activity within CPD is one of the issues that both projects examine. However, the projects differ in context and culture. The American one is teacher led and school focused, whereas the UK project looks at the interactions between school-based research, the needs of teachers and the input HEIs can make. However, similar issues and areas of concern are raised when considering the concept of CPD.

The case studies attempt to show how collaboration between HEIs and schools can be effective in the continuum of professional development. What is clear from both studies is that collaboration needs to be constructed and developed over a period of time.

The American case study

The American case study is taken from the National School Reform Faculty Program (NSRFP) which is based in a comprehensive urban high school in southern California. The NSRFP is part of a much larger national American project which is based at The Annenberg Institute for School Reform at Brown University. The Annenberg group have developed a model for school-based CPD. Christelle Estrada is responsible for running this project at the Californian High School. Christelle describes the nature and purpose of the project and the effects it has had on the teachers involved, the school and herself as project leader. She highlights areas that have caused concern, by drawing on teachers' comments and responses. She suggests areas that require further investigation as well as showing us the need to understand the contextual and cultural limits placed on CPD. She draws conclusions as to the effectiveness of the project so far on those involved and the potential effect it has had on student learning.

The American case study highlights areas that cause equal concern in England and as such provides a useful comparison.

The English case study

The English case study is taken from a school-based curriculum development project offered to schools through Canterbury Christ Church College. The model of curriculum development used was based on action research and offered to many schools. The model was open to interpretation, but was guided by a framework designed to assist schools and individual teachers improve practice and gain a deeper knowledge of curriculum-based issues. The approach described followed the action research model, but was adapted to suit the participating schools and teachers. The adaptations were made in collaboration and consultation with the schools involved in the project, and included addressing issues such as research methods and investigative skills, the consequence of which has shaped my thinking on school-based professional development and the concept of 'collaborative partnership'.

The project has been running for five years. It began in September 1992 with five schools taking part, two of which form the main focus of discussion in this book.

The Ashford School-based Curriculum Development Project

Canterbury Christ Church College offers teachers in school the opportunity of long-term professional development through a portfolio system. This was first devised to enable teachers to accumulate evidence of work being conducted in their school/department in a systematic way through 'personal reflection' and 'action planning'. The portfolio is submitted for accreditation purposes. The accumulation of credits was (and still is) a great motivating factor for the participating teachers. The Advanced Diploma is divided into three modules, A, B and C; each is seen as developmental and giving experience in the processes of reflection and action planning. Modules A and B are portfolio submissions while Module C is a dissertation based on reflection, action and academic reading. If all elements are passed sufficiently well, the teachers have the opportunity to continue to Masters level studies.

The aim of the school-based project as specified in the portfolio handbook is: 'to support curriculum development in the school. It enables the senior management of the school to identify the priorities for development, and provide support for teachers who engage in curriculum development work' (p.1). The handbook goes on to give a clear view of the aims and direction of the scheme within a school context, indicating that curriculum development is seen as an enquiry and evaluative approach with two central features:

1. to promote the professional development of participants, and
2. to enable participants to achieve recognition and credit for their curriculum development work (p.1).

The scheme itself is based on an action planning, enquiry model of curriculum development whereby:

'Participants are invited to pursue their curriculum development aims through a process of enquiry and evaluation. The portfolio provides a framework for the collection of evidence of such curriculum research and development. Participants are encouraged to engage in the systematic enquiry and reflection through partici- pation in group activities, and carrying out of curriculum development work.'(p.6)

The original scheme was modelled on an 'action research' framework, with the portfolio structured to support the process of:

(a) taking professional action;
(b) conducting systematic enquiry;
(c) reflecting on the experience.

This framework was the starting point of the project. Participation was purely voluntary, with the deputy headteacher being designated the line manager of the project within each school. Their role was to ensure that the areas of the curriculum and the school issues which the staff investigated were appropriate to the school development plan. The involvement of senior management was a way of showing the school's commitment to the project. The project began in September 1992 to coincide with the new academic year.

The school research groups

These included teachers from various departments in the school, each having different professional needs and areas of expertise, ranging from newly qualified teachers to senior teachers and deputy heads. The main focus of interest was to extend their working knowledge of identified areas within the curriculum, to enhance the teacher/learning environment they worked in, as well as to gain a higher qualification that would help them in their career path. It is pertinent at this point to indicate that many saw this combination of aims as an opportunity of particular benefit in professional development. It was seen as a realistic way of working with the senior management of the school while still attempting to fulfil personal goals and aims. The areas under investigation included:

1. A school induction programme for new members of staff.
2. Attainment Target 1 in the maths curriculum.
3. The nature of a school's professional mentor, with respect to initial teacher training requirements.
4. Assessment of Attainment Target 1 at Key Stage 3 (age 13/14) in the science curriculum.
5. Developing a music curriculum for year 7 (age 11+).
6. The role of evaluation in business studies for year 11 (age 16).
7. Records of Achievement; evaluating their introduction to the school.
8. Assessment of Attainment Target 1 at Key Stage 4 in the science curriculum.
9. Community Studies for exams.

Nature and context of meetings

The research groups in each participating school met five times a term (after school) for seminars, discussions, group inputs and taught sessions led by a tutor (in this case myself; I was the researcher) or a member of the group. The sessions started by introducing the teachers to the idea of enquiry and reflection in the context of the type of questions needed so that planning could take place. This introduction took the form of asking the teachers to provide an initial statement of where they thought they were presently in terms of their roles, responsibilities and professional development. They were asked to focus on the issues which concerned them, giving possible reasons for that concern. Having identified these areas, they were asked to construct a development plan which was submitted to the school line manager and the tutor for consultation: the line manager considered its appropriateness to school issues and policy, and the tutor its academic rigour and accuracy. The teachers were encouraged through group and individual discussion to examine their development plans and refine them into detailed action plans that could be implemented and revised as appropriate throughout the following academic term.

Group sessions were initially devoted to discussion of the processes involved in curriculum development through action plans and development plans. However, increasingly the teachers asked for specific inputs on research methodology, such as how to investigate, formulate questionnaires, gather data, analyse data and build evaluation into research work, as well as for more specific issues of subject content. The teachers were encouraged to keep journals of their progress, by logging details of specific action points taken and commenting on their successes or failures at the time, giving possible reasons for such judgements. To help focus ideas, individual tutorials were given by the line manager and the tutor throughout the term. At the end of the first term the teachers had to submit an audit report and critical narrative (based on personal reflections), of the development work they had undertaken to date.

The second term began with each teacher presenting their work to the group, followed by a discussion so that views could be exchanged and new ideas advanced. Dissemination and discussion were aimed at teachers sharing methods of enquiry as well as involving cross-fertilization of ideas from various departments in the school. It was hoped that this interdisciplinary perspective would help staff to develop a more liberal approach to other departments' viewpoints and to reflect constructively on issues raised across the school. The year ended in the production of the portfolio (Module B) which contained evidence of:

- initial development plan;
- action planning;
- reflection;
- evaluation;
- participation in group activities;
- summative report of the enquiry undertaken.

Of the original 22 teachers, four did not complete the course. The remaining 18 gained passes, with 14 of these gaining sufficient grades to take their work through to Masters level. All 14 teachers continued with Module C, with three new teachers joining the project at Module B level. This created additional problems to which I will return later.

Module C involved a greater commitment from the teachers, making demands both in and out of the classroom in terms of the depth of research and reading required by them. The basic format for the completion of Module C was the same as B, but the depth of academic reading and argument required was significantly greater. The final product of Module C work was the submission of their dissertation. Thirteen teachers completed and submitted their work, gaining sufficiently high grades to allow them the opportunity to continue and gain a Masters degree. Eight have to go on to MA work, four submitting their dissertations at the end of 1996 and the remaining four submitting them in 1997.

Describing the research framework

The study was about research in relation to school and HEI practice. It was not intended to be purely practical, but was concerned with research that would make a difference to the ways in which people work and think about their work, and the way they relate to others. The study was also concerned with questions of methodology, thus requiring an argument to connect the choice and practice of particular methods to the way that the problem was conceived and the utility and limitations of the outcomes.

To understand the nature of the curriculum development project under investigation, which included the contexts of the contributing institutions, the teachers, their worlds and their actions, a qualitative methodology was adopted. This allowed the researcher/tutor to understand the situation as it was constructed by the partnership. It attempted to capture what teachers say and do, that is the product of how they interpret their involvement. The task of the study was to capture this process of interpretation. To do this required an empathic understanding of the feelings, motives and thoughts behind the actions of teachers (Bogden and Taylor, 1975, pp.13–14).

As such, the research assumed a posture of 'indwelling' while engaging in the study. Indwelling is taken to mean existing as an interactive spirit or principle, and to exist *within* as an activating spirit or force (Polanyi, cited in Grene, 1969, p.160). Simply, this can be interpreted as being at one with those under investigation, ie understanding a viewpoint from an empathic rather than sympathetic position. Polanyi expresses this idea clearly:

> 'To this extent knowing is an indwelling, that is a utilisation of the framework for unfolding our understanding in accordance with the indications and standards imposed by the framework... if an act of knowing affects out choice between alternate frameworks, or modifies the framework in which we dwell, it involves a change in our way of being.' (Grene, 1969, p.84).

This statement allows for what Dewey (1934, pp.100–101) considers to be the function of reflective thought, which is: 'to transform a situation in which there is experienced obscurity, doubt, conflict, disturbance of some sort, into a situation that is clear, coherent, settled, harmonious'.

Although Dewey's quote is taken out of context, it does suggest that the outcome of reflective thought is coherent thinking that is harmonious and can be dealt with. However, Schön (1983a) puts forward an alternative view. He suggests that the outcome of reflective practice is 'uncertainty':

> 'As the professional moves towards new competencies he (sic) gives up some familiar sources of satisfaction and opens himself to new ones. He gives up the rewards of unquestioned authority, the freedom to practice without challenge to his competence, the comfort of relative invulnerability, the gratification of deference.' (p.299)

Dewey's and Schön's descriptions of reflection offer teachers, teacher educators and researchers the opportunity to consider what they are involved in or undertake to do. Both interpretations of reflection are important and necessary aspects of teaching, researching and professional development, provided they are seen to be continuous processes. Being a researcher and tutor on the curriculum development project required me to be involved in the collection and interpretation of information gained from the project, as well as tutoring the individual teachers. This meant I had to rethink and reformulate the meanings gained from both the data I had collected and the experience that I had undergone with the teachers involved.

To evaluate, reconstruct, reformulate and reconceptualize possible future collaborative frameworks, it was essential for the study to reconsider the meanings given by participants, and to be placed firmly within the context in which they were constructed. At the centre of this assertion is Bakhtin's (1986, p.7) view that: 'If a subject is to be understood, then the relationship between the researcher and the other person must be a dynamic and mutual relationship'. Bakhtin refers to this as dialogue; a dialogue which is open and not dialectic, one which is relational. He sees the researcher as being involved in dialogue or interactive interchange with those who are the subject of the research, implying that each has an effect on the other. For collaborative work to occur successfully and be sustained, Bakhtin's view cannot be ignored. It must be reflected within the methodology chosen for the study.

The case studies put forward here use the above philosophical underpinnings of qualitative research as a way of discovering the meaning of a collaborative framework.

Focus of the study

The general focus for the study was to establish those features which were connected to inter-institutional collaboration. Generalization of the results is not the primary aim of the study, rather it is gaining a deeper understanding of what constitutes participating in collaborative initiatives. Thus the study needs to be placed in context.

Context of the study

The move towards collaborative ventures was brought about through Circular 9/92 (DfE, 1992). Our institution took up the challenge of partnership through ITE and linked to it the notion of CPD through school-based projects. It was aimed at encouraging schools to join the partnership with a view to obtaining ongoing INSET. This whole approach raises questions but is neither the focus or context of the present research. What is important is that the agreement to collaborate by participating schools was a joint venture, and as such the ensuing collaborations offer us the context for discussion. The natural setting of school was chosen for the study as this seemed to be the most likely place to uncover issues of interest and discussion. A critical feature of indwelling is that the researcher spends extended amounts of time with those involved in the project. This allows for the development and fostering of both tacit and explicit knowledge of those involved and the context in which they are working. This is implicit in the chosen methodology as much of the evidence that was to be collected was teachers' and researchers' words and actions. The study had to capture both the language and behaviour of those involved. These were collected by participant observation, in-depth interviews, relevant documentation and group discussions.

The research design was on emergent format (Lincoln and Guba, 1985). The focus of the study involved an initial sample; the focus was then refined as the data were collected and analysed.

The nature and context of data collected

The data collected from the study were to serve two main functions:

1. to provide formative information about the way collaboration was initiated and progressed;
2. to formulate an understanding of the nature and context of collaboration within CPD.

The essence of good information-gathering lies in the reason or purpose for collecting that information. As has already been discussed it was essential that the study captured the language and behaviour of all involved in the project; doing so would allow the aim of the study to be achieved.

Aim of the study

The aim of the study was to gain a clearer understanding of what may be regarded as a framework for collaboration, by considering the intentional interactions between schools and HEIs. To achieve this aim the following questions needed to be considered:

- How were the two institutions to collaborate?
- How was collaboration to be implemented?
- What arrangements were to be made to establish the collaborative process?
- How was the evolution of this collaborative approach to be monitored?
- How and by whom were priorities established?
- How were difficulties to be identified and addressed?
- Could any factors be identified that would show the soundness and effectiveness of the collaboration?
- Did teachers' personal knowledge bases increase effectively?

These questions formed the framework of analysis. The work of Resnick *et al.* (1987), Sirotnik and Goodland (1988) and Schlechty and Whitford (1988) proved valuable sources of information for such a framework. They showed how institutional interactions could be viewed as a model of practitioner-research.

Using the questions above based on the Resnick framework, data were collected from five primary sources, over a period of three years; the timetable is shown in Table 4.1:

- guided interviews with the practising teachers;
- the project programme;
- participant observation;
- teacher evaluation sheets;
- research journal.

Table 4.1 *Timetable of the data collection*

Nature of data	1992	1993	1994	1995
Interviews	Summer	Spring	Summer	Spring
Project programme	Autumn	Autumn	Autumn	Autumn
Observations	Ongoing throughout the year	Ongoing throughout the year	Ongoing throughout the year	Ongoing throughout the year
Evaluations	Spring/ Summer	Spring/ Summer	Spring/ Summer	Spring/ Summer
Research journal	Ongoing	⟶		

The information-gathering process

Interviews

The interviews were structured so that all participants (including the school line manager for professional development) were involved.

Most of the interviews took place while I was the participant observer. The interviews took on an informal approach through guided questions, allowing the interviewees freedom of response. In this way the interview data were perceived as what Mishler (1986) terms a 'form of "discourse"'. It allows for a depth of conversation in all areas of concern to be stated. This was a crucial element in establishing collaborative relationships built on trust and the acceptance of mutual differences.

Participant observation

Participant observation is a qualitative data-collection method that allows the researcher to understand people's lives and actions in *their own terms* by spending extended amounts of time with them in their own natural settings, in this case the teacher in their own school. It also allows for a description of the cultural aspects of a teacher's working environment. By being a participant observer both in school and HEI, I attempted to understand, using Polanyi's terms of indwelling, how both institutions appeared to operate and work together. The broadest approach was taken by asking both institutions:

What is happening here?
What is important?
How best can you describe what is happening within the context of collaboration?

This method allows for the simultaneous combination of document analysis, interviewing of respondents and informants, direct participation and observation, and introspection (Denzin, 1987, p.183).

The information collected was categorized under the following headings:

- Evidence of the scheme enhancing professional development.
- Evidence of institutional issues being involved.
- Evidence of collegiality and collaboration of the group affecting outcomes.
- Evidence of the type of input required to meet the needs and demands of those involved.
- The nature and context of the reflective process.

The research journal

The research journal is seen as an integral part of the research process (Glaser and Strauss, 1967). The journal represents a personal record of insights, beginning of understandings, questions, thoughts and discussions that took place during the five years of the project. It has proved to be an invaluable source of information.

Considering the issues

Professional development

The criterion for selecting evidence of professional development was the degree to which individuals were able to show, through their own planning, implementing, evaluation and reflection, that they were able to improve their practice, personal knowledge and understanding of the concept of change within the context of the problem they were investigating. Evidence was also required of the impact on curriculum development, whether on a departmental or whole-school level.

Generally the teachers found reflection of this nature both difficult and taxing. They viewed it as a form of self-criticism. However, with encouragement and support they began to think and act in terms of:

- asking the right types of questions;
- planning a set of actions that would facilitate the investigation of a set of problems in a systematic and cohesive way, based on a sound methodology and knowledge base;
- evaluating their own results in a way that allowed them to consider alternative ways forward and the appropriate actions to take.

Evidence of this development was to be found in their portfolios, in which action plans became more articulate and specific. Evaluations became more rigorous and reflections were less self-critical, but more analytical and revealing in the areas where they felt further development was required. The teachers began to show evidence of formulating and developing their own theories, reinforced by the skills required for such development. A good example of this is a concluding point from a portfolio submission:

> 'It appears therefore, that in the current context, coherence at the "macro level" i.e. as established within the present central government funding arrangements, and in the absence of a school development plan, is difficult to achieve. This has encouraged the development of a "reactive" (seeking to solve immediate problems), rather than "proactive" (enabling inventory practice), approach.' (Webb, 1994)

These formulations were articulated more accurately through the collegiality of the group.

Institutional issues

These were some of the whole-school issues addressed in the summative documents of the portfolios submitted by individual teachers.

The most interesting feature of the research was to be found in school 1, where several teachers, each from differing departments, were considering Attainment Target 1 of the National Curriculum (practical assessment). Through the group discussions it became evident that each individual's department was attempting similar things in this area of the curriculum (the general consensus was that the wheel was being reinvented!) However, the successful outcome of these discussions was the cross-fertilization of ideas and the calling together of all departments involved in Attainment Target 1 within the school, so that a common approach to the assessment could be developed and implemented. Similar curriculum-based developments that affected whole-school issues were to be found in school 2. A member of the group was looking at assessment within her own department and what effect this had on assessment across the school. The conclusion of this work is in process: the school is considering assessment procedures in an integral way, by taking account of staff opinion and giving acknowledgement to individual teachers for the work being done in particular areas.

Another example from school 2 shows how, by enquiring into and developing an existing school policy of information technology, general classroom effectiveness can be improved. IT was to be delivered in the school in a cross-curricular way. This had been a senior management decision, but very little attention had been given to the monitoring of skills and levels of attainment of pupils, or to staff expertise to deliver IT in order to meet the statutory requirements of the Dearing Report (1994). One teacher developed profiles that were easy to follow, both for staff and pupils. This was achieved through interviewing staff, pupils and senior management teams in order to establish the needs, levels of expertise, and hardware and software requirements for the school. This enquiry has led the senior management of the school to reconsider the demands it makes of staff who may not be able to deliver IT as first intended. The follow-up work for this teacher will be to look at how best the school can meet the needs of teacher development in IT skills. Academically this piece of work will constitute his Module C.

Collegiality and collaboration

Group dynamics often call for (or rely upon) subjective comments, and this was a fascinating category to observe and record. The first set of sessions in each of the two schools was relatively quiet, with individuals trying to establish what was expected, not only from the project but from the other members of the group, as these comprised the most junior members of staff as well as senior teachers. Initially input was made retrogressively, with the senior members of staff 'pulling rank' by experience. This gradually disappeared as the group began to ask questions about the reasons for having conducted particular practices at the school for so long. Questions such as, 'Is this still applicable now?', 'On what criteria was that decision made?', 'Is there appropriate evidence to substantiate claims?' were increasingly asked and, more importantly, discussed openly. It was this integration of ideas that increased the collegiality and collaboration between the participating members. It also became evident through their portfolio work that collaboration was extending to everyday practice. The journals of those teachers who felt confident showed that they found it important to work together and discuss relevant issues. They stated clearly where members of their groups facilitated the enquiry work by setting up meetings or taking questionnaires to their departments, thus ensuring responses were obtained. It must also be said that some members did not find integration quite so easy.

Meeting individual needs

Teacher needs were an evolving aspect of this project in each of the two schools. As tutor and researcher I had specific duties and responsibilities. My first concern was with delivering the course according to the portfolio guidance. Second, I needed to collect information and data in order to evaluate the effectiveness of the course in meeting institutional requirements.

In effect, my evidence of teacher needs became a list of requirements imposed by the teachers. These included skills and methods associated with research and inquiry that they felt were necessary to complete not only their academic work, but to develop specific areas of the curriculum. Teachers expected me to understand these needs and deliver the type of information and support they required to make their enquiries successful. Understanding and appreciating such contextual differences was a significant learning experience for all involved, especially when the process of action planning and the ideas of curriculum development and the management of change were not ones they found easy. Each of these areas required specifically taught inputs as well as additional support material, so that the teachers could experiment with such ideas to acquire a deeper understanding, and hence to implement some of their new knowledge. This process was essential if the teachers were to progress from Schön's reflection-in-action to reflection-on-action.

Time and support were the teachers' requirements, both from the school and the tutor. The more supportive schools allowed teachers to have cover for individual tutorials; in these cases teachers were very proactive in their work. For the tutor the demands made were often far in excess of the time allocation from the HEI, causing a conflict of interest.

Teachers found a school-based environment a very useful way to combine professional development and school development; although they were not always seen as synonymous, the teachers did appreciate that they were inextricably linked.

One of the most noticeable aspects of this project was that the teachers involved felt the need to develop professionally. It can be argued that the teachers on this course were so self-motivated that they would be involved in professional development irrespective of whether it were school-based or not. However, I would suggest that not all the teachers gained as much from this approach as they might have done from a more formal taught Diploma course; on the other hand, many made gains which they might otherwise not have achieved.

Dean (1991, p.67) suggests that:

'assessing needs involves identifying areas in which it is possible to improve performance... some experienced teachers may find it difficult to accept the idea that any part of their work needs development.'

This has certainly been true for the two schools. A more formally taught course would certainly have allowed some of the teachers to use other research methodologies.

Reflections

The notion of critical reflection as described earlier, drawing on Habermas (1971), Giddens (1989) and Schön's (1987) view that reflection is concerned with a critique of the social structures within which people act, has been of direct importance to the focus of this study. The school-based approach enables teachers to make sense of events in their schools or classrooms by discussion or writing. It enabled them to make plans for action and to affirm their values. However, this form of reflection, I would argue, is a step closer to action, rather than what Mezirow (1981) considers to be introspection. The type of work conducted by the teachers still stands at some distance from the deliberate movement between action and reflection. In fact I would suggest that many of the teachers were still at the stage of what Schön (1983a) describes as 'the action present'. It seems extremely difficult for teachers to conduct realistic models of teaching whereby they may practise and refine their actions. Real classrooms appear to be too busy places, frequently not allowing the teacher to step outside the continuous action in which he or she is involved in order to make sense of what is occurring and has occurred. At seminar sessions this had been very evident, as many teachers' reflections had been on events of problematic interest rather than on theoretical improvement. Discussions were often at a very concrete level, interpreting events and incidents, suggesting possible solutions to immediate problems.

Success or failure?

The school-based project as described here has had its successes and failures. Why? The limitations of the projects fall into two distinct categories, one attributed to the nature of the project itself which was methodologically bound, and the other to what I have called 'strategic implications', which involve cultural and contextual issues. The most significant aspect of the project's success lies in the effect it has had on the teachers' personal views of their own professional learning and development.

Methodological issues

The portfolio is based on elements of enquiry, action research and reflection. In the educational literature this type of process is described by Carr and Kemmis (1986) as a 'self-reflective spiral of cycles of planning, acting, observing and reflecting'. They also describe how action research should take place, linking it with critical interest and reflection, and defining it as:

> 'a form of self-reflection enquiry undertaken by participants in social situations in order to improve the rationality and justice of their practices, their understanding of these practices, and the situations in which the practices are carried out.' (p.162)

In this definition, self-reflection is seen as bringing about emancipatory and social change. Bearing in mind that the action research framework is not easily introduced to schools, because teachers have to learn and to understand the process of self-reflection before they can effectively carry out such research, it is beneficial if the school and staff believe in the fundamental philosophy of such research. I was very fortunate that such a philosophy was acceptable in the majority of cases, and allowed to develop in such a way as to promote further development in the two schools: this might not always be the case in similar projects. In fact, within this project, the limitations of action-based inquiry as portrayed in the curriculum development project were often discussed, and staff frequently asked for alternative methodologies to be considered and explored. Action research might not always be the correct approach for the outcomes sought by the school. It would be wrong to make teachers believe that action research was the only way to enhance curriculum development; equally it would be unethical to say that it was the only approach to successful professional learning and development. This type of project has the potential to be successfully implemented in many schools: however, a greater flexibility needs to be considered if we are to involve teachers in process models and collaborative research. Teachers need an understanding of the mechanisms of change within a firm knowledge base for true and lasting development to occur. It is essential that teachers are allowed to see and experiment with various curriculum methodologies and philosophies, in order to analyse and evaluate their practice systematically.

The curriculum development project described here focuses on what Schön (1983a) calls reflection-in-action, and in particular what he calls the 'reflective conversation'. This is a process of conscious on-the-spot experimentation in the present action, which occurs when practitioners try to resolve the unfamiliar problems confronting them in their professional practices (pp.26–31) The two schools involved in this study have extended the duration of the project in their respective schools to allow the teachers to continue their research and curriculum development, and extend their reflective skills. Some have progressed to Masters level while others have joined the group at Diploma level. This type of long-term professional learning and development has been continually monitored in a systematic way over a period of three years. The data that have been collected so far have allowed me to evaluate the effectiveness of teachers' personal learning and the impact it has had on the school development plan, as well as shape my thinking on the nature and contexts of collaboration initiatives and the concept of 'collaborative partnership'. The most positive and encouraging observation to date from this particular project has been that the approach can produce effective professional development, implement change, and improve practice in the way described in the opening statement of this chapter. However, part of the success lies in the open communication between participants and the acceptance that each participant has a view as valid as the next.

Strategic issues

The time allocation, as stated previously, is imperative to the success of such a project. It is very time-consuming for the tutor attached to a particular school. As first envisaged the project placed a great deal of emphasis on the individual teachers to produce their action plans, etc on their own. This is an over-estimation of what can be expected of teachers setting out on such a project for the first time. (It highlights the cultural gap between schools and HEIs.) It is also an over-estimation of teachers' understanding of the principles of change and their implications on direct classroom practice. A great deal of input is required from the tutor to explain the reflective, action research approach. As part of such a programme it is necessary to introduce teachers to ways of investigating the types of questions needed and the types of data collected, as well as the nature and context, and use of action plans. Frequently the work to be considered needed theoretical input before action planning of any nature could take place. Despite the investigations going on in their classroom, the teachers asked for direction and theoretical alternatives. As their confidence grew their questions became less pragmatic and more knowledge based; the nature and context of their enquiries became more analytical and developmental. These facts cannot be ignored if one is thinking of embarking on such a joint project. The teachers required continual encouragement, despite the collegiality of the group and working environment. When working a full day, with all the pressures of a teaching job, teachers found it difficult to continue this type of enquiry and professional development; it was not a lack of commitment on their behalf, rather cumulative pressures. It is for this reason that the tutor's role is paramount in supporting and enhancing the experience, as well as in continually encouraging the teachers to complete their work. The success of the project lies in working in true partnership with the schools. To quote Watson and Fullan (1992, p.219):

> 'a strong partnership will not happen by accident, good will or establishing ad hoc projects. They require new structures, new activities, and rethinking of initial working of each institution, as well as their inter-institutional workings.'

I think the above quote is fundamental to collaborative ventures between schools and HEIs. Certainly from the school-based curriculum project I have come to learn the importance of building such relationships, and the value of them once they have been established. Re-thinking institutional and inter-institutional workings is the key to successful 'collaborative partnerships'.

What can be learnt from the project?

Professional development is difficult and demanding: it requires effort, time and opportunity. In order that collaborative enquiry and individual professional development can occur, those involved must accept responsibility for working in collaboration and partnership. What does this mean and how can we address the issues?

What is it to collaborate?

The introduction to this book highlighted the need for teachers to be able to extend their own personal knowledge base when involved in professional development. It also indicated that over the years many and varying approaches have been implemented, all of which have relied on funding being available from the government or local education authorities. This has meant schools and teachers being involved in the type of professional development that could be considered 'imposed'. So what is different about a collaborative approach as described in the school-based study? Teachers need the autonomy to decide how and in what area they wish to develop. They also need to feel that they have something to offer the educational world. In the past many have felt a great divide between the university researcher and themselves. The culture of each institution has been, and is, very different (and made explicit in Chapter 2), making the concept of collaboration difficult. Sirotnik (cited in Goodlad, 1993, p.31) suggests that:

> 'School systems and university systems are not cut from the same cultural cloth. The norms, roles, and expectations of educators in each of these educational realms could not be more different, e.g. in the regiment of time and space in the school vs. the relative freedom of these precious commodities in the university setting.'

He considers it to be a 'culture clash'. Cuban (1992) takes this argument further, suggesting that researchers are known primarily for their publications and professional standing. He bluntly argues that:

> 'The notion that professors and practitioners are engaged in the same enterprise, sharing common purposes, has been shredded into finely chopped specialities, distracting dichotomies such as theory and practice, and an abiding hunger for higher status by increasing the distance of scholars from public school classrooms.... In being known, we have gained a crippling rigour in our research and kept potential colleagues at arm's length.' (p.8)

If this is the case, where does collaboration and a collaborative approach fit with my study of the practitioner-research scenario? I would argue that the descriptions put forward by Cuban and Sirotnik are valid and accurate in certain contexts, but not all. In recent years there has been a significant movement away from the approach mentioned above towards the teacher researcher. A recognition of the required roles, responsibilities and difference in attitudes has been reported by Young (1990), McNiff (1993) and Hargreaves (1995).

The present study was a definite attempt to move away from Sirotnik's description. As previously stated, the project was based on the implicit assumption that practitioners and researchers would learn from each other, and that this could only come about through intentional collaboration and partnership. Four significant areas emerged in establishing a sustained collaborative framework: initiation, implementation, monitoring and evaluation.

How was the collaborative approach initiated?

Collaboration was initiated in two ways: first by making a needs analysis of the teachers' requirements and the HEI's contribution to those needs. From this it was evident that the teachers required pre-specified knowledge and skills that would facilitate an understanding of the process model they were working in. Planning the year ahead together allowed for the development of existing leadership skills and enabled both beginning and experienced teachers to work more effectively with their institutions. It also strengthened the platform of partnership. Establishing needs from within with HEI collaboration helped erode the scenario of schools waiting for an HEI 'expert' to tell them why they were required or the HEI waiting for schools to tell them what the school wanted. The problems were negotiated laboriously. At this point it was also evident that the project had significant research potential and that this would be progressing alongside the project. Both parties accepted the difference in potential roles and chose to continue with the project.

Second, formulating a research methodology (described earlier) with which the participants were happy allowed both teachers and researcher to work collaboratively. This involved the teachers and senior staff having a strong voice in what they perceived curriculum development to be, and the nature of the inputs required from the HEIs to help them formulate such developments. From the researcher's perspective this formed an essential component of the study. The school-based curriculum development project that involved teachers allowed them to have a 'voice', and thus created a rich developmental environment that enhanced the quality of learning and the nature of the curriculum enquiries that took place. The scenario that ensued allowed the researcher to learn and to become more aware of the problems, issues and possible solutions related to school-based developments.

Implementing the collaborative process

To establish the collaborative process, the teachers and researcher constructed an initial three-year framework. This involved addressing group needs and individual needs, as well as producing evidence of collaborative work.

In both schools, teachers' needs were addressed by an audit which established the area of skills and knowledge required. This was used as a baseline for development. Specific problems were not labelled at this stage as I thought it might set teachers on a preconceived path, or possibly on an incorrect or harmful path, thus inhibiting possible future alternatives and achievements.

My thoughts here were influenced by Dewey and Schön. However, it is interesting to note that from the 24 teachers audited, all mentioned feeling insecure with research methods, enquiry-based work and what constitutes research.

The introduction to these issues is an area of study that is often ignored or omitted in school-based teacher research projects. It is an area that I feel is crucial to teacher development and as such requires significantly more attention. If teachers are to understand what it is they are investigating, and thus improve practice, they must have a clear conception of the nature of enquiry and be able to devise strategies to implement the enquiry. It is not that teachers cannot research; they can! What they require is the tools to do it with, so that improved practice can be sustained. Teachers and researchers need to openly discuss these issues if collaborative frameworks are to be implemented and sustained. Veal *et al.* (1989, p.331) suggest that it is essential 'to encourage teachers to discuss their learning needs and to seek help requires a supportive atmosphere that does not exist currently in many schools'. I would say that the same may apply in HEIs. How can we change or modify if we do not understand?

To meet the needs of the teacher, five formalized sessions per term were organized. These looked at issues such as the management of change, curriculum development, research methods, and data collection. Interspersed with these taught sessions, which took place after school but on the school site, teachers had two set tutorial-type meetings with the tutor. The teachers frequently asked for more support, and where possible this was given.

The three-year framework was built in a progressive line. Teachers were not forced to see their commitment as three years, but there was increased motivation with obtaining an advanced Diploma; thus the majority did see this project as long-term professional development.

Interpersonal relationships were important in implementing the project. Understanding of difference is a prerequisite of success. The tutor/researcher by their mere presence in the school constituted an intervention in school life; altering what occurred while in the school. However, within the collaborative framework, it was clearly established that the tutor/researcher, although bringing new ideas and expertise to the school, did not provide a specific direction for the schools' development plans, but provided a platform for teachers to work and research collaboratively within the school.

Monitoring the collaborative process
It is essential that any collaboration is monitored to establish its value. The research methodology previously described how the collaborative process was to be monitored through indwelling. However, the teachers also had a significant role to play. Each teacher kept records of the sessions they attended and in which they participated, logging areas of tension or problems

they encountered as they conducted their work. These proved to be a rich source of material for discussion at interviews and a way of evaluating the project at the end of each year, and over a period of years.

The end of the project for each teacher was the submission of a portfolio of curriculum development at levels B or C. Each portfolio described and analysed an area of investigation and development undertaken by each teacher. Through systematic analysis of the problem and the collection and evaluation of evidence, the portfolios showed how the teachers had increased their knowledge and skills relating to research methods, curriculum issues and possible solutions to problems. The quality of the work submitted for assessment was significant, with 22 gaining merit for their work.

Evaluating the collaboration

Fullan and Hargreaves (1991, p.37) have claimed that 'schools are not now places where individuals and collaborative growth of teachers can flourish'. To some extent I would agree with this statement, particularly as it applies to an individual being isolated in his or her classroom, making collaborative decision-making difficult. This conclusion is similar to that of Johnston and Hedemann (1994). However, I would disagree with Fullan's statement when taken in the context of the research community; here there has been a positive collaborative approach between the school and the HEI. Teacher, school and researcher have developed professionally through the collaborative approach. Teachers as individuals have acquired a greater understanding of the enquiry process, and the researcher has become more aware of the nature and context of school-based development. The schools have gained by the implementation of innovative curriculum development. The researcher has been able to evaluate and produce evidence for possible ways of reconstructing school-based programmes, which further enhance the nature of long-term professional development for both communities. This assertion fits Young's (1993, p.252) findings that teachers found it easier to collaborate when dealing with broader concerns rather than those related to strategies for teaching in individual classrooms. Hargreaves (1991, pp.53–4) suggests that true collaborative relationships are spontaneous, voluntary, development-orientated, unpredictable, and persuasive across time and space. This may well be the case within schools, given the difficulties that teachers are faced with in their administrative roles; I have not found it to be the case in collaboration between the two communities of research and teaching. The main barrier is how this type of work is conceptualized by one's colleagues in both institutions.

A framework for collaboration

To summarize the project, a framework for collaboration is suggested here, based on the successes and failures of the project.

In the past, the culture within the research community and that of schools has made the notion of collaboration difficult (Sirotnik, cited in Goodlad, 1993). Roles and expectations have been very different. Fullan (1993) pointedly states that, 'if one of the most prominent heresies of educational change is the culture of individualism, then collaboration and collegiality are pivotal to the orthodoxy's of change' (p.186). This argument is particularly suited to the present situation in the long-term professional development of both the teaching and research communities.

Structured collaboration between HEIs and schools can form significant planks of policies to restructure both communities in terms of courses developed, learning outcomes and long-term professional development needs.

A framework for collaboration requires:

- a working relationship that is allowed to evolve and is sustained through the trust of the teacher/researcher environments;
- the belief that working together is not through compulsion, but is voluntary and is valued among the two communities;
- that development of skills and initiatives is seen as an ongoing process whereby change can be implemented and supported;
- that working together is seen as a scheduled activity which gives status to what is being developed, but does not stifle the individual's own development;
- an open appreciation of the needs of those involved: there must be no hidden agenda.

Collaboration cannot be enforced, nor can it rectify the division in the theory/practice framework. What can be aimed at is a culture of mutual learning, whereby each educational community can support and enhance the quality of teaching/learning outcomes. I would argue that when collaboration is seen as promoting professional growth, institutional improvement will ensue.

Conclusions

Two major conclusions result from my involvement in this project. One is that collaboration must be grounded in mutual trust and respect, reflecting equity among the participants. The sharing of learning is an evolving process, allowing a knowledge base to be created with respect to curriculum research, development, and a collaborative framework. The second is the need to understand what it is to work in genuine collaboration rather than cooperation. Participating within a partnership requires the individual to put in a great deal of work and effort in order to craft an effective and sustained collaboration.

To move towards such a collaborative environment requires changes in both types of institutional culture. Teachers' work needs to be more valued, and researchers need to be more adept at researching the needs of teachers within the theory/practice divide. The precipitation of such a notion would be a synthesis of a teacher education course equipping teachers with skills and knowledge beyond classroom use.

The American Case Study: *Christelle Estrada*

This case study describes and analyses the interactions of ten teachers participating in the National School Reform Faculty Program (NSRFP) in a comprehensive urban high school in southern California. The Annenberg Institute for School Reform at Brown University has developed a model of school-based, continuing professional development.

The purpose of the NSRFP is to improve student learning by developing reflective practitioners through 'collegial communities' (AISR, 1995, p.1). There are two major components which support the development of these communities: first, educators, trained by the institute as coaches, who will assist the group members in developing specific skills that support reflective practice and second, administrators, both at the school and district level, who actively support professional learning communities within the school. Both the school and the Annenberg Institute contribute financially to this initiative. The school provides release time for the teachers during the monthly meetings, that is, monies for substitute teachers. The Institute provides stipends for both the group and the coach and creates opportunities for ongoing training at summer institutes, and regional and national conferences for all the coaches as members of the national faculty.

The following case is divided into four sections: a description of the context of the study; an explanation of the research method; a description of the interactions of the Annenberg group; and a collaborative analysis which was synthesized by the group's coach.

The context of the study

The school's student population is approximately 2,100: 5 per cent Asian and Pacific Islander, 39 per cent Latino, 31 per cent African American, 25 per cent Caucasian (48 per cent of the latter group being of Armenian heritage). For 30 per cent of the student population, English is a second language: one-third of these students (10 per cent of the total population) are designated Limited English Proficient (LEP) and two-thirds (20 per cent of the total population) are designated Fluent English Proficient (FEP). The student population is divided into four smaller structures called 'houses' or schools-within-schools. Three of the houses have a team of teachers for each grade level, ninth through eleventh. The team consists of teachers for maths, science and humanities (English and history). Seniors, twelfth graders, are connected to the house by the counsellor who provides both guidance and career advice. A resource teacher works collaboratively with the counsellor and assists teachers in ongoing professional development. The fourth house is a special programmes house which includes The Center for Independent Study, a drop-out prevention programme; the special education programme for students with special needs; and two business partnership academies, one focusing on graphic communication and the other on the visual arts.

The research method

Phenomenology is the theoretical basis for the research design used in this case study. According to Moore (1991, p.94) phenomenology is a method of 'reflecting on experience and letting conclusions emerge from those reflections'. Using the works of Husserl and Merleau-Ponty, Moore asserts that this method is an attempt to understand intentions within a specific context through explanations offered by participants themselves.

The foundational epistemological assumption of this case study is that individuals can understand human action through language and that personal accounts of one's perceptions reveal one possible view of experience in a specific context. The method of enquiry, as characterized by Geertz (1973) in his *Interpretative Theory of Culture*, does not begin with a governing principle of hypothesis within which a series of observations takes place. Rather, generalizations emerge from specific actions within a specific context. Consequently cultural theory is not predictive, that is the projection of outcomes from experimentation, but instead is the construction of interpretations. The aim then is to draw large conclusions from what was said and done over the period of a year in order to support broad assertions about the role this particular group played in creating opportunities for reflective practice of its members.

Data used for the case study are selected memos, responses from a questionnaire used as feedback for a national conference, and portions of the minutes from the two-hour monthly meetings conducted during the 1995–96 academic year. The focus will be twofold: how the group established a professional learning environment; and what the group said about the experience of peer observations.

The theoretical framework of the interpretative analysis is based on the ethogenic method as explicated by Harre and Secord (1972). There are three levels of analysis:

1. Actions. Looking at people's perceptions and their interpretations of actions and environmental conditions.
2. Persons. Looking for the source of power in their personalities.
3. Speech. Looking at what is said when it accompanies actions.
   (Moore, 1991, pp.15–16)

Copies of the case study were sent to members of the Annenberg group and they were asked to respond to two guide questions: based on what you read in the case or from your experience in the group, what words or phrases would you use to describe how the Annenberg group exemplifies collaboration? From the case, what are some of the issues (insights or challenges) that seem to emerge when thinking about the idea of collaboration within a school context for ongoing professional development? The responses from the group members were then analysed based on the frequency of comment. Similar comments were clustered together and then descriptive labels were created to identify relevant conceptual categories. The analysis was then submitted to the members of the group for comment and further revision.

The role of theory in this case is to provide language with which to speak about the concept of collaboration as it is manifested in the actions and words of a particular group of educators. In other words this enquiry is shaped by key underlying questions: What is the meaning for the teachers of their own actions and worlds? What does this knowledge (ie, their own understanding of their actions and words) show about the context in which it is found, and more than that, about larger issues in ongoing professional development within a school context?

The interactions

In September 1995 the principal distributed a memo to the faculty explaining the school's involvement in the Annenberg project, inviting interested teachers to become members of the group. The explanation made it clear that the project was based on research which showed that improved classroom practice and student learning are most likely to occur when there is a collaborative work environment. The expectations and level of commitment were clearly outlined for the faculty. The memo stated that each member must:

- meet for two hours each month with the group;
- develop a professional portfolio;
- participate in peer observations at least once a month; and
- make a two-year commitment to the project.

Ten teachers, including the coach, committed themselves to the project. The group consisted of three males and seven females; three humanities teachers, those teaching an integrated English/history course; two house resource teachers and the bilingual resources teacher, all teaching social studies to students whose first language is other than English; two maths teachers; one science teacher; and an English language development teacher. Of the ten teachers five were involved in the bilingual and English language development programme. Three other teachers on the faculty expressed interest, but were either near retirement or felt over-committed for the year and commented that the younger teachers should have the benefit of the project.

The group met informally over lunch at the end of September to establish the meeting day and time. Six of the ten teachers taught classes at seventh period and needed substitute teachers, since the requirement was that the group meet two hours each month. Teachers received the agendas at least two days before each meeting and at the end of each meeting the agendas were generated by the group based on the commitments made to the Annenberg Institute. At the first meeting the group considered four major questions:

1. What kind of professional environment do we want to create for our group? (Norms of discourse and professional expectations.)
2. What process and schedule will we create for our peer observations? (At least once a month.)
3. What do we want our professional portfolios to be for us? (Function, process, product, standards of excellence.)
4. What criteria will we use for disbursement of funds?

At the first meeting the group established commonly agreed norms and expectations. They were:

'Be punctual. Let members complete ideas. Avoid interruptions. Let each person speak for self. Be patient with each other. Be aware that people are new to this work. Be forthcoming, direct, honest. Be critical – that's why we are here. Be supportive and respectful. Focus for two hours: be here. Be committed to each other's professional growth.'

At the first meeting the group also agreed some procedures:

- The group would use consensus for decisions.
- Facilitators would rotate every meeting.
- A designated observer, focusing on particular areas identified by the facilitator, would conduct the debrief at the end of the meeting which would be open to all members.
- If anyone had reservations, concerns, or simply wanted to rethink or revise any procedures each person should feel free to call a time-out to look at what was happening.
- Refreshments would be provided by each member. If people wanted to be reimbursed they would let the coach know.

At this meeting one member asked about the group's relationship to the school community. The consensus was that what happened in the group would be communicated informally and when the group was more established memos to the faculty would update them on the group's progress. These more formal communications could include, 'Topics for discussion which might be of particular interest to the faculty, specifically professional portfolios'. It was agreed that meetings would be open and people welcomed as observers, although the expectation would be that they would 'not jump in unless they were invited to participate and understood the established norms'.

At this October meeting the group focused on the processes and logistics of peer observations, and questions about the professional portfolio and disbursement of funds were postponed until the November meeting. Two teachers, with the input of the group, created a matrix for scheduling observations. After the matrix was set up, based on each person's conference (preparation) period, each teacher designated the particular class he or she wanted to be observed and the observers were selected based on who was free to do so. In a specific instance one teacher wanted the two members who had the most experience of teaching language minority students to observe her class. The other members showed no preference for who observed them; consequently, cross-discipline observations were the norm. For example, an English teacher and a social studies teacher observed a science teacher or a maths teacher and the bilingual resource teacher observed the ninth grade humanities teacher. At that first meeting the selection of classes to be observed was discussed. Several members selected the class that was the most challenging for them:

'The processes for the peer observations were created by consensus.
The teacher being observed will set the agenda for the two observers:

– Think of questions on which you want the peers to focus.
– Remember this is to help you. Shape the observation the way you want it to help your practice.

The teacher being observed will make the contact with the peer observers.

– The peer observers should take notes.

The debriefing will be arranged by the teacher being observed and the peer observers as soon as possible within at least two days of the observation.
    The teacher observed should be in charge of the feedback session: asking key questions.
    One of the peer observers should lead a short debrief session about how the feedback session went: What was helpful? What was not? Comfort level should be foremost.'

At the second meeting there were adjustments made to the common expectations for peer observations. The group agreed that: 'It is the responsibility of the one being observed to not only set up the observation and the focus, but also the debrief so that the feedback can be more immediate, within the day of the observation'. Some people thought that the debrief of the feedback session was not helpful. One person suggested that it was too difficult 'to go into a touchy, feely mode'. Some felt that it created 'a safer environment.' The coach suggested that one reason for having an observer in the feedback session was to make sure the environment did not become 'adversarial' with people feeling 'intimidated or defensive'. The consensus was that: 'Whoever is being observed can settle the process for how the debrief happens'. After the first set of peer observations three models of feedback sessions emerged and the coach made copies for the members. The models were:

1. The person observed wanted general impressions and then specifics from the check-off sheet provided for the observers.
2. The person observed begins reflecting on the lesson and then the peer observers respond to their colleague's observations.
3. The person observed specifies three general areas for comment:
   - general goals and design of the lesson;
   - what engages this group of students;
   - suggestions for modifying the lesson or the learning environment.

Throughout the year a part of each meeting was designated for feedback from both formal and informal observations. At the December meeting the facilitator, a humanities teacher, made a general comment contrasting the first with the second peer observation debrief done by the group: 'The first time seemed to be very general and this time really focused on students and the learning outcomes'. During the first series of peer observations the most common statements were:

'I felt validated. It was different from administrative observations which is a part of their job. It was weird when we went to other rooms... what I was doing was important to the observers. There was mutual support, being able to see both sides. When kids act crazy or every kid is not engaged that it's not me or just me.'

'I was really nervous. My ego was on the line and it all revolves around class management. I was thinking: What are the kids getting away with today. I felt uneasy pretty much the entire period. But then at the debrief it became clear that the observers were not being judgmental... this is what I saw you doing, this is what we saw the kids doing. It was framed as "Next time when you do this think about this and this...." It didn't seem like criticism.'

'It was very positive. I am in dire need of assurance and I felt validated and helped out. I loved having people in my room. I had set it up and they saw what I did. It was just extra information for me to add to my bank and use. Going into other classrooms: it was nice to see that these are problems everyone had to face.'

'Surprising I wasn't nervous. Having someone in that particular class and feedback has made me rethink the class and how I see the class and how I deal with them on a daily basis, not so stressed out as I was before. It's not just me, but the combination of kids in the class. Wonderful suggestions, need to find ways to implement. The criteria I set out helped accomplish that as well.'

'Just having people watch carefully was very helpful. Talking afterwards was interesting because I got perceptions that I couldn't see because I'm going around to groups. I get discouraged about the things I want to fix or make better, making things more relevant and organizing post-experiment work. It was neat to observe the same kids with another teacher. To see how students react. I felt like observing others helped me so much.'

'The experience of going in pairs was very powerful because the observation of the other person was fresh and helped me look at new ways of observation. Being observed by two colleagues was one of the best teaching experiences of my career. I realize that in the middle of my teaching I'm doing so much intuitively and not realizing what I am doing. This was very helpful and validating.'

'I was really nervous. Observing was difficult to have happen. I was glad for the debriefing, the perspective on the kids. I learned a lot about myself and how I am growing.'

'It was a pleasant experience. I have always enjoyed people coming in. I'm used to people coming in and giving me ideas. I pretend that they're not there. Observers were in my classroom talking to the kids. In the debriefing it focused on my goal of independence for every child, more self-reliant, not always dependent on the teacher.'

At the next meeting, during the next group debrief, the focus was on student learning.

'I talked to the kids in the class, sat down and asked them: Why are you doing this? How do you get help? The experience of observing to see what the teacher tries to do and what the kids are doing is interesting.'

'I wanted to make sure that the students were doing what I asked based on my ability to move them through a debate protocol. And I wanted the observers to focus on the students' ability to present logical arguments based on evidence.'

'The students were themselves… I wanted to talk about why they were themselves. It was good to have people in the room to see and have concrete ideas afterward. I try and try, but it is in a vacuum, I need other eyes to help me get a perspective.'

The next set of observations were informal as well as formal. Two teachers worked together and team-taught essay writing in an English language development class. The teacher whose class it was said: 'We helped the kids get through the outline and it was helpful because they were used to doing essay writing in English'. Her partner commented:

'We used a writing program that requires that they write on demand. We are trying to get kids to step write efficiently and effectively. The kids had an outline previously that was not working…. We will collect papers and data for the ESL [English as a Second Language] students. They do better when teachers use the same style consistently… it takes them less time because they are already familiar with the process.'

Since it was the end of the semester two teachers had portfolio exhibitions. This process was developed by the ninth grade teachers three years pre-viously. Students in ninth grade humanities classes maintained working folders for their assignments which they kept chronologically. At the end of the year the students selected representative samples of their most significant work and wrote reflective essays about what they had learned and the application of this learning to their lives, with recommendations for the teacher about what would have been more helpful to them as learners. They would then present their work so that peers and outside observers could ask them questions about their learning.

One teacher who had observers in for the portfolio exhibitions said: 'The observers asked questions and the students said that the questions were hard, but they were really good questions…. It was helpful to debrief and look more closely at what I was doing'. The other teacher remarked: 'The observers allowed me to observe the kids' reactions more fully. I also realized that being in this group has helped me with my observation skills, even when I go to substitute in another teacher's class'.

Other teachers who participated in the portfolio exhibitions commented about the portfolio exhibition process: 'The questions made the kids feel more interested in what they were doing. [It helped me see] what questions are appropriate and help the kids think that what they had learned was more real to them'. Another teacher said: 'I realized these students had learned a lot and that the portfolio is an important tool. So I changed the design of the second semester because of the feedback the students gave me in their portfolio exhibitions. I started with debates instead of a simulation'. At the end of the year portfolio exhibitions became the focus of more observations. One teacher said about her own experience: 'When I was observed I realized that the portfolio shows how little they know…. How can we get them to realize the limits of the knowledge? How can I get that point across?' Two first-year teachers commented about the use of portfolios. One said: 'It was helpful to see how questions help the student'; another commented:

> 'I had to learn how to ask questions for the portfolio. They learn things and parts of things so the questions give them an opportunity. It gives them the skill to figure out what they don't know. It was interesting to see how questions can be different and how they produce different results. My students will be doing portfolios and I am interested in what happens with my students.'

At the end of the first semester a questionnaire was distributed to the coach by the Annenberg Institute as data for ongoing evaluation of the group's progress. The responses were then collated by the coach and used in feedback sessions at the national conference with groups of three other coaches. The six open-ended questions were:

1. What do you feel good about?
2. What is positive about what is happening?
3. What seems to be working?
4. What are you unsure of?

5. What do you wish you knew more about?
6. What worries you?

Nine of the ten responded to the questions. Five of the nine responded to the last question, 'What worries you?', and of the five three responses focused on the relationship of the group to the school community. The issue might be characterized in the form of a question asked by a member: 'Do we need the support of the rest of the school?' The other two focused on the 'daily demands of teaching' and how the work of the group might be impacted.

Questions four, 'What are you unsure of?' and five, 'What do you wish you knew more about?' elicited three common responses. The greatest ambiguity centred around questions about the development of the professional portfolio; how we would expand the process to include the school community by creating new groups; and issues of time and ability to work with peers in evaluating student work and more specific teaching strategies. The first three questions could be characterized best by the four following comments:

'I feel great about working with a small group of teachers committed to improving the lives of students.'

'Our group is very focused on effecting change in the classroom; and learning how reflection on our practice is the key to improving our own teaching.'

'The peer observations are extremely helpful and, in fact, invaluable when trying to assess yourself.'

'Our model of decision making [consensus], while a bit slow, is working in our group. The members seem to be comfortable with the decisions we've made.'

Collaborative analysis

Of the ten members, nine responded. Of the original members three would no longer be in the group for a second year. One teacher moved to the east coast, another became an administrator in another district, and the third took a teaching position in a district closer to her home.

Three categories emerged from the words and phrases identified by the teachers: personal qualities; professional qualities; and collegial qualities. Teachers generated words that described personal qualities: trust, integrity, commitment, accountability, mutual respect, openness, honesty, supportive, friendship, patience. Professional qualities were characterized in these ways: self-reflection, continuous analysis and assessment, working together to help each other meet the needs of students, learning how the group can support the school, considering the professional suggestions about changes in the classroom, creative problem-solving, willingness to take on challenges, take risks, work through tough issues, willingness to take and give criticism and then to try to use it in changing/developing teaching practices, acknowledging that others see things that you do not see and taking this as valuable rather than threatening. The term 'collegial' is used as a descriptor for words and phrases that seem to capture what members identified as non-hierarchical structures: shared facilitation, consensus decision-making and democratic involvement. One member attributed the creation of an 'atmosphere of togetherness' to the fact that 'we are all engaged in the art of teaching kids'.

In general one might conclude that for this group of teachers collaboration could be conceptualized as a relationship in which personal as well as professional qualities create a learning environment where shared responsibility is the norm. One member wrote: 'Norms are designed to encourage communication…. If norms are followed then silences stemming from personal conflicts should be worked through before going on. And this is every member's responsibility'. Another member identified the practices of shared responsibility, consensus and rotating facilitation as a way 'to create a situation of real equality' which encourages 'different styles of thought, discussion techniques, and approaches to issues'.

Another general conclusion could be that collaboration, from an educational perspective, is purposeful. In other words, its ultimate goal is reflective practice so that changing teaching strategies improve student learning. The assumption implicit in this statement is that teaching strategies must change based on students' learning outcomes. Consequently, this group of teachers not only values feedback given by peer observers, but by the students as well. One teacher, during a peer observation, summarized this perspective: 'I was asked to talk with the students during the lesson's work session. I learn more from students talking about how the teacher teaches. This way I can learn more about what they can learn and how'.

Emerging issues

The members identified five significant and interrelated issues which provide some insights into the nature of the 'collegial communities'. These issues are: the public nature of the group's work; the positive aspects of diversity; the aspects of commitment in the group; the role of change in reflective practice; and the relationship of the group to the school community.

Two people identified the public nature of the group's practice and its importance in shaping the culture of the group. One first-year teacher commented that the stereotype of the closed classroom was being broken down. For her this was evident not only because peer observers came into her class, but that other members of the school community supported her when she attended the two-hour meetings and needed a colleague to teach her class. Another first-year teacher thought that the commitment of doing peer observations was actually a 'public statement' and therefore created an inherent 'public responsibility' which had two complementary results. First, 'teachers made their classrooms open for a more public assessment'; second, colleagues were more apt to follow through with their commitment as peer observers.

Three people mentioned that the diversity of the group contributed to the group's effectiveness. One teacher suggested that it was the 'diversity that helped the most' because there are limitations to 'specialization'. Another teacher wrote that collaboration between 'different kinds of people' is essential. For this teacher, difference in ethnicity, gender, thinking and teaching styles as well as subject areas is necessary for two reasons: first, the school community is diverse; second, as a group, teachers are learning how to improve their teaching for different kinds of learners.

Five teachers mentioned the issue of commitment related to several areas. Two teachers suggested that the nature of commitment was a key factor in the group's ability to collaborate. One teacher explained: 'This model works well for me because it is a small group of committed people' and they had chosen to be in it. Three other teachers wondered how commitment could be sustained considering the daily responsibilities of the classroom. 'Collaboration is time-consuming and this is a challenge for overworked teachers'. A possible solution is 'to think about collaboration as class preparation because it actually helps one prepare classes'.

Six of the eight teachers who responded connected the work of the group to change in classroom practices. Three of these teachers connected the creation of the group's professional environment with the ability to change actual classroom practices. One teacher explained: 'These processes are ones teachers could strive to use in their classrooms, creating a less hierarchical and more equal setting, with collaboration as a common practice between students and between students and teacher'. Another commented that the creation of a professional learning environment was slow and 'a bit frustrating at first' because the group did not immediately get 'into day-to-day teaching strategies. The value of building effective norms and processes' is now evident to him because it supports 'the more nitty gritty changes' he is considering. He no longer discusses 'specific teaching strategies in a vacuum'. Another member makes a similar connection between environmental factors which support changing practice: 'The group's mission' along with processes need to be constantly clarified 'so that the group is working for all members' and adjustments can be made when necessary. This particular teacher concludes her reflections with two key questions: 'Should the group be posing new challenges to its members? Or do the challenges of teaching inform the group's work?' Perhaps a deeper question is one of relationship. What is the relationship of each member's personal professional goals to the group's goals?

One possible way of looking at this relationship is identified by two other teachers. They connect personal commitment to the process of change. One teacher wrote that in the group, 'all teachers have decided to be involved because they believe they can improve their practice... there are no teachers who feel like they have basically figured everything out already. So openness to change is vital to the success of this kind of collaboration if it is really going to have any effect at all in the actual classroom.'

A first-year teacher seems to validate this line of thinking when she writes: the 'commitment to self-assessment and change within the classroom is a strong force among members in the group'.

For at least five of the teachers peer observing is a key strategy which creates a safe environment as well as the context for the kind of change that would directly affect student learning. One teacher begins her reflection on changing practice with two questions: 'How do we change as teachers? And how does the school change to provide better teaching?' Her answer is that the peer observation model provides her with a 'type of assessment which is helpful for her planning'. She often has the observers speak with the students about their learning. She states:

'The feedback session is invaluable as a way for me to get criticism and ideas and try to use them to change and improve my practice. This is very challenging... I often have to reclarify what I am doing and why and try to concretely incorporate what I have heard.'

When considering changing classroom practice the majority of the members identified peer observation as one way to improve teaching within the school community.

Seven of the eight teachers who responded commented on the relationship of the group to the school community. The word that most often charac-terized this relationship was 'commitment'. Members wondered if implemen-tation on a school-wide basis could happen 'because of the high level of commitment the group requires and ensures'. Three teachers looked at the commitment of the group to the larger school community. How would the group help other teachers experience the value of peer observations? How would the members support new groups in creating their own 'safe' environ-ments? How would the group remain a distinct identity while at the same time encouraging 'school-wide unity'?

A first-year teacher questioned how the group could become more public, 'not a mystery', while another teacher wondered if 'going public too soon and too fast' would produce groups with different agendas. One general obser-vation is that for this group sustained commitment is an essential element in conceptualizing collaboration. One member posed an important question: 'How do we prevent this project from becoming another "passing fancy"?' This is a crucial question in light of the fact that educational reform has been introduced in the United States largely without discussion or dialogue.

In response to this question the group's commitment to the norms estab-lished by the Annenberg Institute is shaping the future direction of the group's work. During the second year of the Annenberg project the members will focus on the development of individual professional portfolios which document each teacher's reflective practice. The group has already created mutually agreed performance standards which will be used by a review panel to assess each teacher's areas of strength as well as the areas of growth. The concept of an exhibition of work to a panel in a public forum is not new to the school. Since the school has been a member school of the Coalition of Essential Schools, an educational reform organization at Brown University, for the last eight years exhibition by portfolio has been one form of assessment with students in the humanities. This is based on the idea in graduate education of a public defence of one's dissertation. At the end of the portfolio exhibition the teacher will become a member of the National Faculty of the Annenberg Institute or, based on recommendations from the reviewers, will concentrate on areas which need continued professional development.

Based on the collaborative analysis by the members there are two key factors in creating collegial communities within schools for ongoing professional development. One essential factor in reflective practice is the personal commitment of individual members not only to their own growth, but to each other's; and this commitment must have a public dimension to it which becomes a shared responsibility not just a personal one. The second key factor is the actual processes used to create the kind of professional environment which takes into consideration a wide range of experience and teacher-generated knowledge. This spirit of 'equality' or 'democratic involvement', as one teacher suggested, seems to happen because of a more profound commitment. In other words, a group with first-year teachers as well as veterans, can collaborate because each teacher is committed to a larger purpose, that is, student learning.

To generalize, one could say that this group's concept of collaboration is based on a commitment to reflective practice because of a foundational assumption, similar to one articulated by Harre and Secord when writing about ethogenic research: human beings have the 'power to initiate change', can perceive more than the self and are aware of that perception, and have the ability to create the language to name the perception (1972, pp.86–95). One teacher articulated this assumption clearly when reflecting on comments in the case study made by his colleagues on the power of peer observation in changing practice. He wrote that it was important to not only acknowledge 'that others see things that you do not' but to also take 'this as valuable rather than threatening'. In this particular group of teachers diversity is valued and as a result the variety of viewpoints expressed becomes an opportunity for learning from each other in ways that help students learn.

Concluding Remarks

The NSRFP project in southern California and the Ashford project in England are undoubtedly different in nature and context, yet both are concerned with CPD. Both projects highlight areas relating to culture, context, hierarchical structures, role, responsibilities, expectations and possible achievements. The interesting commonality is that teachers on both sides of the Atlantic appreciate collaborative partnership, but accept the difficulties that are attached to such commitment.

Christelle suggests that from an educational perspective collaboration could be purposeful, in that its ultimate goal is to allow teachers to be involved in the type of reflective practice that changes teaching strategies and improves student learning. A similar conclusion can be drawn from the curriculum development project. Essential to all areas of CPD has been the desire to learn, develop and achieve, this has come through in both projects. The collaborative approach is one that can benefit all participating teachers, teacher educators, schools and HEIs.

An essential factor in collaborative partnership and success is that reflective practice is seen as a personal commitment by individual members, not only to their own growth, but to each other's; and this commitment must have a public dimension to which it becomes a shared responsibility not just a personal one. This requires teachers, teacher educators and researchers to accept that reflective practice is part of the continuum of professional development and as such applicable to all involved. An equally important factor that has come from both projects is that the process by which a collaborative environment is created is fundamental to the professional development of those involved. It has to recognize and consider a wide range of experiences, cultures, roles and knowledge bases, 'equity' and 'shared leadership' being the baseline.

Chapter 5

A Theoretical Perspective on Collaborative Partnership

Introduction

The previous chapters have considered what it is to work in partnership and how the use of collaboration and cooperation has come to be associated with partnership agreements. Such agreements and ventures require contexts in which to operate, and depend on the social and psychological perspectives of those involved within them. Giddens and Dewey provide a social context to examine partnership and the respective roles of participants within a structured framework; Vygotsky, Bakhtin and Piaget offer a constructive dimension to the way individuals can construct their knowledge within a given context.

Partnership and the constraints it imposes on both schools and HEIs suggest that in order to understand the concept of collaboration and cooperation, within that partnership, a given context is required. The context takes account of both internal and external factors influencing institutions, whether these are OFSTED, government initiatives, whole-institution development, departmental development or individual development, and therefore determines whether the stated aims of the partnership are reached. Some of the factors that influence the nature of collaboration are due to formal structures, management constructs, social processes, and the social construction of knowledge.

Semin (1986) cites Mead, Wiittgenstein, Berger, Giddens and Vygotsky as a way of investigating the interdependent relationship between individual and social processes. One aspect that is of particular relevance is that of the post-structuralist theory. It suggests that the social context allows individuals to make use of opportunities presented to them (Davies and Harre, 1990).

What is particularly interesting and pertinent to the argument is that individuals do not always act out of particular knowledge schema; rather they act into the context of the situation, in terms of the choices that it offers (Giddens, 1995; Shotter, 1988, cited in Shotter, 1992). Teachers frequently attend development days or training courses, not because they wish to do so as part of their own personal development, but because the institution they work for expects it of them or requests them to attend. Similarly in HEI tutors are assigned to research initiatives for reasons other than personal development.

From these examples it is possible to think of collaboration affecting teachers and tutors in two ways:

- social context/demands
- psychological context/individuals' demands/needs.

Social Context

If collaboration is to exist and become effective in terms of the professional development of those involved, both the structure and the culture of institutional collaboration need to be addressed. Existing structures can be inappropriate, obsolete and slow to respond to changing circumstances. Schools and HEIs are not static environments, and are continually changing and developing through identifiable cycles. If this is the case how can inter-institutional collaboration take place? Giddens (1989, 1996) puts forward the concept of 'structuration' which can facilitate such a discussion. His theory suggests that:

> 'people are always and everywhere regarded as knowledgeable agents, although acting within historically specific bounds of the unacknowledged conditions and unintended consequences of their actions.' (1996, p.265)

The implication of this quote is that teachers and researchers are autonomous people working within pre-specified historical structures, ie, that schools concentrate on pupil learning and that universities concentrate on research. Giddens distinguishes between 'structure' as rules and resources, and 'systems' as reproduced relationships. 'Structure' refers to the basic stock of knowledge that people carry around in their heads as a result of living in particular cultures or subcultures. Thus a teacher from school will carry the influence of that environment into his or her behaviour (for example in terms of catchment area, school development plans, day-to-day working conditions). These elements are not consciously talked about, they are simply brought into a person's behaviour without them really being aware of their influence. Giddens refers to this as 'mutual knowledge'. It highlights the need to consider the social processes which create, maintain and sustain such structures within schools and HEIs. Giddens' theory of structures represents both the medium and the outcomes of activity, allowing the individual freedom to be transformative and creative within his or her environment.

Giddens' argument is exemplified within the complex interplay between teaching, learning, research and effective professional development, all of which can (and do) shape the nature and function of collaboration. Within a partnership participants need to display commitment, effectiveness and ownership. This requires them to make choices, and to be reflective in those choices. Giddens (1994, p.126) argues that:

> 'the advance of social reflexivity means that individuals have no choice but to make choices, and these define who they are. People have to construct their biographies in order to sustain a coherent sense of self identity.'

If this is the case, it challenges participants from schools and HEIs to examine where they fit in a partnership agreement and the roles they choose to play within it. Will they be a professional tutor/mentor or will they be a subject mentor? Will they participate in ITE at all? What role will the college tutor have in school-based training? Or with respect to INSET, is the project going to be long- or short-term? Will there be a school-based project leader? Will the HEI initiate and develop the work or evaluate outcomes of the project? The key to successful partnership is that whatever the nature of the collaboration, there is a clearly identified purpose and aim to the venture, one that will be of mutual benefit to all concerned.

Partnership can be and is used as a means of extending existing educational and research opportunities. It is a way of advocating a collaborative framework, ie, partners actively collaborating to promote more effective learning conditions, continuing professional development and overall school improvement. Within this active and interactive involvement, one must not lose sight of the dialogue and trust that needs to be built up in order to sustain the partnership. Most partnerships have a business perspective to them and as such involve a financial commitment. Cost-effectiveness affects all areas of education, especially HEIs which are encouraged to achieve 'efficiency gains' by increasing student numbers or giving greater access to higher education. The school improvement movement has had particular effect on education departments, where the promotion of a wider range of courses, research opportunities and initiatives has been required. This in turn has necessitated greater dialogue between schools and HEIs in order for collaboration to take place. There is a need to take account of the management demands of partnership, and the individuals' capacity to participate within the given partnership arrangement. The school-based curriculum development project, described in the previous chapter, highlights this very problem. The project required management decisions, which in some cases limited the individuals' capacity to participate within the project. This frequently revolved around areas in which the teacher wished to develop, and whether the school management thought this type of development was appropriate to the whole-school development plan. Giddens (1995, p.116) suggests that:

'dialogue should be understood as the capacity to create active trust through an appreciation of the integrity of others. Trust is a means of ordering social relations across time and space. It sustains that necessary silence which allows individuals or groups to get on with their own lives while existing in a social relation with another or others.'

This encapsulates many of the problems encountered when attempting to develop partnership and collaborative frameworks. The acknowledgement that individuals need to have their own space but still be able to contribute to a collaborative project is essential to formulating a successful collaborative framework. This applies both within and between institutions. The Annenburg project, described in Chapter 4, shows this clearly by the commitment teachers made, not only to the in-school observations and meetings, but to submitting portfolios for the HEI. Such development is based on the understanding and accepting of trust and integrity as a way of establishing social relations. Oakeshott's (1991) concept of 'civil association' reflects this well.

'Civil association' allows us to consider what collaborative partnership looks like and depends upon cultivating the 'civil conditions' which are represented in the 'relationship of beings'. This is not a 'process' made up of functionally or causally related concepts: it is intelligent relationships enjoyed only by virtue of having been learned and understood. When teachers and teacher educators understand the relationships they find themselves in, collaboration becomes effective. The comments from teachers in the Annenburg project clearly demonstrate how dialogue and shared learning experiences can improve classroom practice. Central to the success of the project is the notion of 'civil association' as it depends on 'intelligent relationships', ie, living alongside others in a way that respects their autonomy. From an inter-institutional perspective this is crucial to both understanding and accepting the differing contexts in which schools and HEIs have to function. Dewey (1916) argues that 'civic efficiency is neither more nor less than the capacity to share in a give and take experience' (p.20). This element is reflected in the Ashford case study, where teachers required knowledge of research methods before they could conduct their enquiries. The project responded by enabling this to happen. This change or response to demand reflects a positive appreciation of difference, an element, I think, vital to making collaboration work between HEIs and schools. The fact that the research may be of a fundamentally different order to that of the teachers' own work, should not constitute a problem, provided each acknowledges the difference in the type of development and action that is taking place.

Establishing a collaborative framework based on 'intelligent relationships' and 'civic efficiency' requires a context in which to develop these ideas. The theory of 'action' which deals with the relationship between motives, reasons and purposes, by taking account of institutional organization and change, provides a means by which the discussion can proceed. Giddens (1995) suggests that considering action within institutional structures can be problematic to some extent because 'structure has usually been conceived in a fundamental way as a constraint upon action' (p.196). However, he also suggests that structural properties of institutions can also be enabling. In this sense, structure is implicated in people's freedom of action as much as it is in the limitations that it imposes on their behaviour.

What implications has this for working in a collaborative framework? Constraints and enablement have their own implications within a sociological perspective. But, how can they affect what is perceived to be going on in schools and HEIs? In one sense constraint can be taken to mean the things which individuals are compelled to do by external factors and which they consciously decide they wish to do. An example of this is a person wanting to become a teacher; they first have to obtain a degree, then gain qualified teacher status, and then pass an interview to obtain a teaching position. Equally, compulsion can be things that individuals do not wish to do but are required to, such as compliance with the statutory requirements of the National Curriculum at its first inception.

The 1988 Education Act introduced the National Curriculum, national testing procedures and local management of schools, a consequence of which is considerable change and apparent constraint on teachers' working practices. This in turn created substantial interest from researchers, their aim being to understand the constraints and the effects upon schools, teachers, learning outcomes and INSET opportunities for teachers. Research into the National Curriculum and its consequent implications was neither compulsory nor requested at the time, yet HEIs through their researchers wanted to be involved and construct meaning from the changes that had been implemented by schools, as well as describing the methods through which the changes had occurred. (Figuratively speaking the notion of partnership had not yet developed although many schools were cooperating with HEIs to establish data on the changes.)

Circulars 9/92 (DfE, 1992) and 14/93 (DfE, 1993a) introduced major changes to ITE, bringing with them tension between government policy and professional views. The two circulars provided the main focus for change in the provision of ITE and had significant repercussions for both schools and HEIs.

Circular 9/92 states that: 'the planning and management of training courses should be the shared responsibility of higher education institutions and schools in partnership' (DfE, 1992, Annex A 1.2). This highlighted a fundamental but compulsory change for HEIs: schools were to play a much larger part as full partners in ITE. There was to be joint overall responsibility for all aspects of the course. However, within the stated framework schools and HEIs were to accept different emphases. This implies that there is an obligation for both sides of the partnership to make clear the specific components assigned within the partnership agreement. Circular 14/93 sets out further obligations with schools having to play an even greater role: 'Schools should play a much greater and more influential role in course design and delivery, in partnership as appropriate with higher education institutions' (DfE, 1993a, p.5).

Circulars 9/92 and 14/93 do not make it compulsory for schools to partici- pate in ITE training. However, if they decide to enter a partnership scheme, they are obliged to follow government policies. If we consider the introduc- tion of the National Curriculum, it initially constrained schools and teachers; it also enabled researchers to access a considerable quantity of research data on the implementation of a national initiative.

The implications of such constraints have changed the way research in schools needs to be addressed and conducted. Cooperation is still needed but the emphasis has to become one based on trust, acknowledgement of differ- ences and true collaboration. Dialogue should be a central feature of collabo- rative research. What needs to be gained is a level of understanding that reflects the constraints of each institution's aims, practices and work. This will allow teachers and researchers to bring their own particular expertise to a partnership which has the potential to enhance the professional development of all those involved. Such a reconceptualization of collaboration will be difficult, but necessary, if links between schools and HEIs are to be sustained. This implies that schools have to establish a clear view of what it is to be in partnership and how they can make such an alliance dynamic and effective in promoting whole-school development. This is an exciting and provocative challenge for schools to rise to. They must start to consider how they can implement long-term school improvement and the role they wish HEI to play within their planning. Equally HEIs need to consider and establish their future role in school improvement. The way forward is through *collaborative partnership*; it is crucial to the future of HEIs' role in school improvement. HEIs can offer long-term consistent planing and evaluation of quality to schools. They need to recognize the potential value of working closely with schools on specific improvement projects. The very fact that HEIs can act as a 'critical friend' and support improvements within schools needs to be accepted and nurtured in departments of education.

Psychological Context

Of equal importance to the social context is the psychological context which considers the social nature of learning and construction of knowledge. It provides insight into the way learning unfolds as a social act in social settings (Rogoff and Lave, 1984; Vygotsky, 1986), allowing us to look at 'knowing' as a social act (Bakhtin, 1981; Dewey, 1934). An appreciation that knowledge can be constructed in different ways, hence producing different kinds of knowl- edge, leads to the question, 'How do political, historical or social features leave their stamp on collaborative work?' In many ways they leave a significant mark. Schools and HEIs that have worked together for a long time in the context of ITE have found it difficult in some cases to break away from old models of training. Such historical remnants deter positive development. Psychologically old methods feel more secure even if they are obsolete, and when held on to can cause tensions. Essentially understanding how knowledge is linked to learning and the context in which that link occurs, whether it be political, social or historical, influences the nature of collaboration between institutions.

Dewey (1916, p.43) suggests that 'education is not an affair of telling and being told, but an active and constructive process'. This is particularly important when considering what it is schools and HEIs are trying to achieve in terms of teacher education and development. For Dewey education is a creative and constructive activity which is progressive and productive rather than merely reproductive of the pre-existing social order. The significance of this is that if collaborators acknowledge that development requires growth, and growth necessitates change, a more effective working situation may develop with respect to INSET and professional development. This clearly comes out in the Annenburg project where peer observation has allowed teachers to recognize their strengths and weaknesses, and alter their practice in a creative and constructive way. At the end of the year teachers viewed peer observation as an effective and worthwhile collaborative venture. The project highlights what the continuum of development represents by focusing on 'the educative process of growth, having as its aim at every stage an added capacity for growth' (Dewey, 1916, p.59). It is inevitable that if growth is to occur 'intelligent relationships' are required which involve a variety of people. In this way social interaction may take place with the exchange of ideas, the solving of joint problems, and the sharing of inquiry and analysis of specific issues. This gives rise to the notion of an educative community. Such a community developed in the Ashford project, sharing problems and routes of enquiry and exchanging ideas. Dewey recognizes the idea of community, highlighting that:

> 'in any social group whatever, even in a group of thieves, we find some interest held in common, and we find a certain amount of interaction and cooperative intercourse with other groups. From these two traits we derive our standard. How numerous and varied are the interests which are consciously shared? How full and free is the interplay with forms of association?' (p.89)

The last two questions are of value to the debate. How numerous and varied are the interests of HEIs and schools? Equally, how full and free are the interplay and forms of associations between schools and HEIs? These are very interesting and difficult questions to answer. What are schools and HEIs trying to achieve by working collaboratively in the field of professional development? Possibly a naive answer would be, to enhance the quality of education in both institutions. Teachers, teacher educators and researchers are in the occupation of education, which can be considered as a continuous activity having a purpose; then 'education *through* occupation consequently combines within itself more of the factors conducive to learning than any other method' (p.319). Teachers can be given the opportunity to learn through their occupation in the form of school-based research and development. HEIs have the ability to support and accredit such initiatives. It is an element of partnership that HEIs must seriously consider. It allows for a variety of creative and exciting alternative approaches towards collaboration.

The element that needs to be considered here is what is meant by 'meaning' being socially constructed and occupation being important to education. It is an element concerning 'logic', and one that could pose a threat to collaborative partnership. Garrison (1995), interpreting Dewey's philosophy, suggests that the element of logic required infers that:

> 'If the mind and self are indeed made through participating in social practices and, as is rather obvious, social practices, tools and language are themselves social constructions and equally obviously, there can be no denying that power fashions practices and tools into the shape it desires for them, then there can be no doubt that political power can shape minds and selves into the forms those wield it desire.' (p.737)

This implies that learning is central to education and that if meaning is socially constructed, knowledge has to be acquired, but, what knowledge, for whom, and how is it to be acquired? In terms of INSET and professional development programmes, who decides what these programmes will entail? Who will deliver them? Will they be accredited? Are they for the benefit of the institution or the individuals within them? What role will knowledge acquisition play, if any? Before any of these questions can be considered it is necessary to identify how knowledge may be acquired and if indeed it can affect the way programmes are designed and delivered.

Discussions on knowledge acquisition are currently influenced by two views on 'transmission processes', whereby education is defined as a process of transmitting knowledge from an expert to an unsophisticated learner (Bloom, 1987; Rousseau, 1979). This approach considers knowledge to be external to the learner and acquired through a variety of activities such as practising routines and procedures developed by others, most of which are modelled on the experts' behaviour. The main purpose of the transmission model is to transmit and preserve the knowledge base. Within this construct, research is perceived as systematically adding to the knowledge base through rigorous and accepted procedures. This type of learning equates to many one-day training days where information is given out without time being allowed for assimilation. This model of learning has been severely criticized in that knowledge is not passively acquired but constructed by individuals through interaction with people and their environments. Knowledge is conceived as being internal to the learner (Piaget, 1926), and learning occurs through dynamic interactions within a given social context (Bakhtin, 1981; Vygotsky, 1962). The individual's learning is constructed on his or her prior knowledge, which is affected by the individual's personal thoughts and experiences. Teachers experiencing poor pupil performance will only be able to understand under-achievement if they are given the opportunity to explore their conceptions of under-achievement and then change those conceptions in the light of new evidence or experience. In this construct one is less concerned with the transmission and reception of knowledge, and more with the individual becoming aware of the knowledge under construction and with the challenging of that knowledge. Learning is seen as facilitating the individual's own construction of knowledge. The tasks teachers are involved in have to have meaning and context within the realms of their own knowledge; only then will they be able to reflect on their practice with pupils who are under-achieving, and change their strategies to incorporate their new knowledge, skills and understanding. This type of development was experienced by teachers enquiring into science and maths in the Ashford school-based project. To facilitate learning of this kind, research is perceived as providing a steady supply of alternate ways of viewing and thinking about the associated problems.

This explanation of learning and knowledge construction helps put a collaborative framework into perspective. I have suggested that professional development be viewed as a dynamic two-way process between schools and HEIs. My view of learning reflects this statement in that I subscribe to learning being constructed by the individual. I am concerned with exploring the kinds of strategies, relationships and contexts that can facilitate teachers' and researchers' knowledge construction in educational settings through the context of professional development. Of particular interest is how teachers and researchers inquire into school-based issues, and develop from that experience.

HEIs have a fundamental role to play in this context. Supporting teachers in understanding the process of learning and how this affects practice and ultimately raises pupil achievement should underpin collaborative ventures between schools and HEIs. It implies that teachers need to learn how to describe their current understandings, inquire into other possible interpretations, then reflect on what they have learnt before implementing any changes to their practice or situation. Describing and writing are facets normally associated with research, so psychologically do teachers require this expertise? Dewey (1934) suggests that expertise resides, like knowledge, within the individual. This fits well into the collaborative framework argument, as Dewey (1916) also sees that 'civic efficiency is the capacity to share in a given experience' (p.20). If expertise lies within the individual, but the individual needs to be made aware of this, then what better way than sharing experiences through mutual dialogue? Working collaboratively in this way promotes expertise and knowledge, allowing learning to be thought of as a continuous and steady improvement of practice.

A practice that becomes aware of issues and problems, as well as having the expertise to identity ways of clarifying and addressing them, allows expertise to be seen not as storing knowledge, but as experience, empirical data and knowledge which can join together to produce a creative and effective environment for development and change. HEIs' role is to support such development through collaborative partnership. Schön's (1983a, 1987) work on the reflective practitioner shows us how uncertain individuals are when placed in unfamiliar settings. He suggests that:

> 'contrary to mythology, we are largely unable to "know" in situations of social change, if criteria of knowledge are those of the rational/experimental model. The constraints of knowing affect not only our ability to gain certainty, or precise knowledge, but our ability to establish knowledge in the rational/experimental model at all.' (1971, p.201)

HEIs can limit the uncertainty by working closely with teachers within their own schools. Uncertainty is an everyday situation in which teachers find themselves in the classroom. 'The world we live in today is not one subject to tight human mastery... it is one of dislocation and uncertainty' (Giddens, 1994, p.3). This implies that problems arise and solutions have to be found, and the most effective route has to be applied. This fits well with Dewey's (1934) notion of the 'problematic uncertainty', as founded in problematic situations, and is essential to inquiry. To improve in any area requires teachers and teacher educators to accept there is a 'problem', however large or small this may be. 'Problematic uncertainty' enables teachers and researchers to pose questions and find possible answers to them through enquiry. A typical question could be: 'Does low achievement exist in my class/school?' While the problematic raises notions of conflict and struggle, this can be interpreted as exploring colleagues' ways of doing and understanding. Schön's description above suggests that all problems and situations are open-ended with no definitive solutions that can be imposed from without. This reflects the ideals of true collaborative work. Both interpretations open up alternative ways of thinking about collaborative partnership and continual professional development.

Using Social and Psychological Contexts to Build a Collaborative Framework

Using the social and psychological contexts to discuss collaboration suggests that schools and HEIs have to reconsider what continual professional development means within their institutions and within inter-institutional collaboration. This will require change from both parties. The HEI tutor, teacher educator or researcher will no longer be able to assume the role of education expert, as this causes a division between those who create knowledge and those who use knowledge. Recent work by Bickel and Hattrup (1995) reinforces this argument. They suggest that:

> 'Effective collaboration requires shared leadership and breaking out of traditional roles and relationships. Nowhere is this more important than the need to revisit the traditional approaches to knowledge production that promotes researchers as knowledge generators and teachers as translators.' (p.47)

Placing teachers as translators assumes the transmission model of learning, thus disadvantaging and constraining teachers from entering a meaningful dialogue, and reducing their position of equity within the collaboration. However, teachers do need to feel more comfortable and able to participate in a wide range of social and intellectual skills, knowledge bases and interactions with researchers. Where does this leave inter-institution collaboration in terms of INSET, research, award-bearing courses, school improvement and continual professional development? Here again I must return to the differences between educational institutions.

Professional Development and INSET

The terms 'professional development' and 'INSET' are often used loosely and interchangeably. Both are used to describe a large variety of activities that are specifically designed to increase teachers' knowledge base. INSET frequently refers to the courses teachers attend, whether these are external school-based, award-bearing or skills-based. Professional development is most often seen as moving teachers forward in their own personal knowledge and skills, and can be considered as a form of professional learning. This is the fundamental approach taken here. Within this context it is relatively easy to talk about INSET and professional development as a matter of course. However, this would be a mistake as there are considerable implications for both teachers and teacher educators that require consideration. Day (1986) noted three areas of constraint which can affect teachers' responses to professional development:

1. external factors affecting the climate in which professional development may flourish
2. social and psychological factors affecting responses of teachers
3. the kind of leadership roles and strategies used by the leader.

Although these points were made ten years ago, they are still very valid and relevant today. These three issues have further consequences, if professional development is to have value for those involved. Teachers need to be aware of what change involves and how it may be implemented effectively. Day suggests that teachers use the following ways in which to avoid the challenges that change through professional development brings. I feel they are still very important points schools and HEIs have to address. They include teachers:

- adopting the language of change but retaining their old behaviour
- becoming selectively inattentive to information that points to problems
- changing jobs or changing their roles within the same institution
- making marginal changes to their behaviour
- using authority to elicit the desired behaviour from others, so that they conform to the desired changes.

These factors significantly affect the outcomes of professional development and INSET initiatives; collaboration or collaborative partnerships can make them more effective. In order to understand the nature of this effectiveness it is necessary to point out that individuals bring their own values, attitudes and assumptions to situations which involve change and possible development. They also have needs which affect their underlying assumptions about their involvement in development initiatives. Day *et al.* (1987) identify the following areas:

- affiliations – the sense of belonging (to a team)
- achievement – the need for a sense of getting somewhere in what is done
- influence – the need for a sense of having some influence over what happens in the work setting
- ownership – the need for a sense of personal investment in the outcomes.

These four areas are articulated in each of the case studies. Ownership of the project is important to all participating teachers and tutors. A sense of achievement is an ultimate goal, whether it be in the form of better practice in the classroom or the development of an effective induction programme. Acknowledging the identification of such areas highlights the complex nature of professional development and the continuum of learning and improving. This situation can and often does become more complex if the professional development of the HEI tutor/teacher educator/researcher is considered in parallel. Both teachers and HEI tutors have individual views and objectives, stemming from their own particular interests, values and assumptions. I think it would seem fair to say that these 'different perspectives' may well affect the way collaboration is viewed and the readiness with which each party wants to get involved. For individuals to develop, and in so doing improve the learning environment they inhabit, requires two underlying conditions:

1. the knowledge that a course of action is correct
2. a sense of empowerment, by believing that a course of action is worthwhile and possible.
   (Adapted from Wise *et al.*, 1985)

These conditions may well appear different to schools and HEIs; however, they do allow for alternative and creative projects to be developed and implemented.

Working through INSET

What does it mean when institutions work through INSET? The notion of serving needs and establishing criteria for such needs requires exploring. Frequently cooperation not collaboration between institutions takes place, indicating a need to conceptualize what schools and HEIs are actually trying to do. It is also important to clarify the aim of professional development. Who is meant to benefit from the process?

A school perspective

A school's function is generally considered as being one of educating pupils, and as such school improvement is often regarded as improving the quality of teaching and learning for the benefit of the pupils. Hewton (1989, p.37), suggests that: 'A common overriding aim often found in policy documents is that the purpose of staff development is to enhance the quality of pupils' learning'. This would seem a perfectly reasonable aim, especially given the pressure schools are now under with respect to OFSTED inspections and the quality of pupil learning. However, schools also house teachers who need to learn and develop in order to achieve this aim. Institutions depend upon the quality of the working environment to sustain their employees (Argyris and Schön, 1974; Goodlad, 1983; Sarason, 1982).

Acknowledging these points recognizes that professional development can be thought of as having two basic aims: to enhance the quality of pupil learning within the school environment; and to benefit the teachers who are responsible for facilitating learning within the school. Achieving these aims requires schools/teachers to assess their needs. Eraut (1987, p.30) suggests that: 'the profession as a whole and its capacity to improve the service is dependent on the quality of its needs assessment'.

Successful school development therefore requires a specific attempt at identifying and meeting teachers' professional development needs. Legislation over the past ten years, including Circular 6/86 (DES, 1986), has directed schools to develop a coherent professional development policy and structure, with a designated senior member of staff to coordinate the process. The aim has been to provide support for individual teachers and to be prescriptive in recommending specific INSET activities that would determine the success of the schools' professional development policies. Where has this left schools? Monitoring of INSET provision (Harland, 1990; Harland and Kinder, 1991) suggests that off-site professional development courses during school time continue to be the most popular developmental activity. Is this the most effective way of approaching INSET? School Development Coordinators (SDCs) have to match the provision of INSET with the identified needs or requirements of the school/individual teacher. To do this effectively, the SDC must identify appropriate 'providers'. For the first time schools have been able to choose their providers from a variety of sources including LEAs, consultants, HEIs, advisory services and industry.

Through this choice in provider, schools have also looked to more school-based and school-focused INSET requiring delivery on site, rather than releasing teachers for day or week courses. This in turn has led to the expansion of the INSET market, where school improvement and school effectiveness have become 'buzz words' that all involved are trying to understand and achieve. As Hargreaves (1994, p.96) notes, 'although we have an increasingly clear picture of what effective schools look like, we are not very clear about how to create and maintain them'. Schools can now choose, so where has this left the HEI?

The HEI as an INSET provider

The emergence of school-focused INSET and the concept of INSET courses as 'packages' has had to change, forcing HEIs to consider what it means to be in a 'buyers' market'. HEIs also found themselves having to consider Circular 40/87, which stated that:

> 'Preliminary indications are that authorities are planning to make less use of higher education in 1987–88 than previously. The Secretary of State… is concerned that relevant expertise in these institutions… should be utilised to maintain and improve the quality of training.' (DES, 1987, para. 5)

This, in conjunction with the 'CATE criteria' stating that university/college lecturers required recent and relevant school experience, forced HEIs to reconsider their role in teacher education. It became very evident that change was required. Initially the CATE criteria formed an opening whereby schools and HEIs had to cooperate more closely on school-based ITE work. The positive aspects of this were that this new-found cooperation allowed clear objectives and a more focused dimension of professional development to emerge in school-based in-service work.

The continuum of professional development

I started this section by asking the question 'Who is meant to benefit from the INSET process?' In an ideal world the answer would be: all those involved in the process. Can this be achieved? I think it can but it requires considerable change from both schools and HEIs. There must be a fundamental move towards collaborative partnership. But what can HEIs provide now and in the future? Before this question is answered there is a need to consider the role of professional development in INSET.

Professional development can be considered from a variety of perspectives, many of which have more recently been structured into a number of models and frameworks. A major contribution has been made by Ray Bolam (1986; 1995) and is of value to the present discussion. Bolam identifies five basic areas of consideration based on a continuum of learning that meets both individual and institutional needs. At one end of the continuum the individual's needs dominate and at the other the institution's needs dominate; this is shown in Figure 5.1. Within the institutional needs he includes:

- staff/group performance
- individual job performance
- career development
- professional knowledge
- personal education.

Institutional needs				*Individual needs*
1	2	3	4	5
	slight dominance of institutional needs over individual needs	slight dominance of individual needs over institutional needs	dominance of individual needs over institutional needs	personal needs

Figure 5.1 *A continuum of needs*

Bolam's model allows us to consider how professional development can be directed towards the individual and the institution. What does that mean in terms of collaboration? If we consider the continuum and regard 1 as dominated by the institution, this could be a whole-school training day about a whole-school issue and which involves all staff. The issue may require specialist input or school-based workshops. At the other end of the continuum we can consider 5 whereby the individual teacher is concerned only with their own personal growth. This may involve them registering for a Masters degree, or a Certificate course with a given personal specification; it may simply involve reading new educational material. If collaboration exists or is developed these initiatives can be designed, developed and planned for together; HEI tutors can and should learn in tandem with their teacher colleagues.

Bolam's model concentrates on institution vs the individual, which is one of the main reasons I feel it has great strength in a collaborative framework, as such a continuum allows both to be viewed together and individually.

There are contrasting models which could also apply and that merit discussion; one in particular is that of Bradley (1991), although his model also recognizes that individuals' and institutions' needs for development are different. He suggests that the aims of development should include:

- making people feel valued for the job they are involved in
- enabling people to do their job well and receive feedback that is essential for job satisfaction and motivation
- helping individuals to anticipate and prepare for change within their working environment
- encouraging individuals to derive excitement and satisfaction from their involvement in change
- making individuals feel willing and competent to contribute constructively to the development of the institution.

Bradley draws on the fact that there is a significant contrast between individual needs and institutional needs at two levels. One is simply between the individual and the school, the second between the individual and departmental or team needs. This is an important element to recognize, as it requires an understanding of the role the individual and institution play in professional development. Priorities of institutions as a whole will generally reflect the nature of learning provisions on offer to those within that institution. Departmental needs often reflect the provision of specialist learning, whereas individual needs are reflected in the professional role taken on by the individual and how they manage that role and the learning that takes place within it.

The implication of the above is that individual needs and institutional needs have to be addressed if effective learning and improvement is to take place. It is precisely this issue that has caused and is still causing a dilemma in developing effective professional development initiatives. Funding is being reduced, or re-allocated, through a variety of government directives that make schools target specific priority areas. In effect this constrains the type of development one might like to initiate. However, I feel that if a more collaborative approach is taken between schools and HEI it may be possible to target areas of development more effectively and successfully. So what can HEIs offer schools?

What can HEIs provide?

Survival is the name of the game, and HEI departments of education have to deliver INSET to be cost-effective, so where can and do they fit in the scheme of school/individual development?

HEIs deliver INSET in a variety of ways including:

- courses that offer qualifications for individuals to varying levels of sophistication; accreditation can be obtained from Certificate to PhD level
- lecturers may be asked to input to specific school-based days; they may be introduced as the 'expert' in the field, bringing an objective view to the issues under discussion
- frequently HEIs are asked to work with groups of teachers on school-based projects; these may be action research groups, self-evaluation exercises, development of IT skills, or management issues. School-based initiatives of this nature are usually award-bearing and long term, to make them economically viable.

Each of the elements that the HEI can deliver have usually been negotiated at a cooperative level, schools stating what they want and HEIs trying to deliver. This format has considerable constraints and is one that has affected HEIs significantly.

Despite the introduction of recent and relevant experiences through CATE, the 'credibility' gap between the HEI's 'expert' and the chalk-face teacher continues to exist. Often schools are exasperated by the differing perceptions of what school-focused/based INSET should comprise, and whether the HEI has the appropriate resources to deliver the product. Extending this argument, teachers also complain that general courses such as taught Masters and research-based tasks often lack applicability to individual school requirements, with one of the major criticisms being the difficulty in transference of learning to a classroom or whole-school situation.

Schools also find the research element of an HEI's role difficult to assimilate into school-based initiatives, the difference in emphasis often not being acknowledged, with frequent referrals to the ineffectiveness of a 'cascade' model of dissemination. The model has often been seen as a way of linking off-site and school-based INSET. It entails sending one or two key individuals to be trained in specific areas then returning to their base institution and disseminating the key issues they have learnt. This can be on a variety of topics or issues, as well as at a variety of levels. At one level it has involved SATs training in 1991 in both England and Wales; at another level, individuals may attend longer award-bearing courses on school improvement, school development planning, or curriculum development, and on completion or during their course disseminate their findings and knowledge to the wider audience of the institution.

The cascade model requires certain key elements if it is to be operational and successful within an institution. HMI (1988, para. 3.2) identified five areas:

1. the audience be well defined and their particular needs carefully targeted;
2. clear training objectives are set and the training materials are of high quality, well structured, logical, credible and consistent. Detailed and comprehensive training notes, common to all involved, are used;

3. the trainers are carefully selected for their support of the aims of the programme, the match between their experience and expertise and particular stages of the training programme; their competence as trainers; and their understanding of the knowledge and skills to be imparted;
4. each stage of the programme provides time for trainers to prepare thoroughly and for trainees to absorb and reflect on the training;
5. the risk of idiosyncratic personal interpretations of the training objectives is minimised by setting each stage of the whole process within a firm structure and removing any ambiguity in the objectives and the training materials.

Point three has the most significance for collaborative INSET. Cascade models rely on showing participants how to run training sessions, disseminate information and communicate to peers and colleagues. It also necessitates material and resources to be developed and produced to facilitate the process of accurate dissemination. If change is to be implemented following training, support is required over a period of time. Such a major commitment on behalf of individuals is considerable, and often untenable. This is an area in which HEIs can establish a new role. A school or consortium of schools wishing to be involved in this type of initiative should work collaboratively with HEIs to develop resources and training material and to train those teachers who will disseminate the information and skills within their respective schools/ departments. Schools can identify their areas of weakness where they require training and development; by working in collaboration with HEIs alternative models and approaches to the identified needs can be designed and implemented. In this way the collaborative effort is tailor-made to meet the needs of the school or consortium of schools.

Schools and HEIs should design and plan such development together so that materials, resources and support are built into the model. The nature of the cascade would then help whole-school improvement as well as individuals' development, through staged involvement. Those involved gain accreditation for their work, thus making their future role within school development more creditable and acceptable to their peers. Equally, HEI teacher educators would develop through first-hand experience of schools and school improvement issues, and hence gain greater credibility for school-based work and research in the future. The nature of this collaboration opens new and creative ways for schools and HEIs to work closely within the school improvement framework. It is a role HEIs can fulfil and schools would welcome the idea of working towards long-term goals and development.

The HEI perspective

HEIs depend on research and teaching, and INSET and school-based projects are often seen as a way of addressing both requirements. It is this very point that often causes tension between schools and HEIs. Schools are often left feeling that research is done to them as opposed to being involved with the researcher. This leaves a dilemma of how INSET and professional development can be better understood and made more effective if no research is carried out within the context of the school. If professional development initiatives are to improve, research into such development is not only necessary but a prerequisite of HEI development.

This involves a value stance towards development, and the generation of theories for future development and action. Grundy (1994) suggests that the responsibilities of the organization to provide structures which enable rather than impede reflection upon practice are essential to development. She was discussing action research within a school context; a similar argument can be used for research and professional development. Within the HEI the prime role and responsibility of the teacher educator is to provide alternative ideas, theories and views of professional development, and teaching and learning strategies. Without research this would not occur.

What needs to be addressed is how such activities can take place without alienating teachers and teacher educators both within their own institutions and those within which they are working/researching. Day (1995) states this problem quite clearly: 'the crux of the matter resides in the nature of relationships between the external researcher and "subject/s"'.

Part of the solution to this problem can be found in the psychological theory put forward earlier, in that learning is constructive in nature. If the relationship between teacher/educator and teacher is built on mutual respect and allows for a 'deep understanding that is directed towards reconstruction of previously held constructions' (Lincon, 1992, p.381), through dialogue, then it can be argued that the teacher/educator/researcher is more in line with professional development and the extension of knowledge. The active construction of meaning allows the researcher to develop further insights into the role of professional development within INSET provision.

Ultimately schools wish to improve and HEIs have a fundamental role to play in that improvement, not in isolation, but working collaboratively with schools. Research has shown that school improvement relies on:

- setting long-term goals for improvement
- balancing these goals and maintaining quality
- managing the context of the improvement
- strong leadership to allow the above to happen.

The HEI's role within this context relates to the translation of school goals into effective day-to-day practice. The strategies by which schools translate policies provide the link for teachers and pupils to operate. Schools and HEIs that work collaboratively can make these translations more effective by directing senior managers, departments and individual staff towards strategies that will enhance performance. At a departmental level HEIs could help monitor the reviewing of targets and the setting of new targets, the monitoring of pupils' progress by learning outcomes, and evaluate those strategies that schools felt were a priority.

This supportive role is attainable in a market place in which schools control their own finances and are able to choose their own methods and agencies. Schools can exercise their powers in the choice of in-service provision, school development planning, teacher appraisal, new teaching strategies, and whole-school achievement initiatives.

Collaborative partnership allows on-site training in a variety of forms. The advantage of this is that it nurtures and transmits effective knowledge which helps change to take place in a systematic and coherent way. Both the Ashford school-based project and the Annenburg project reflect this type of success. Certainly the two projects demonstrate how HEI contributions can effectively allow teachers to view change as part of their own development and job. It is not a question of 'empowering' the teacher in a patronizing way; on the contrary, the exciting part of the Ashford model is that through discussion and enquiry, change was understood, not as something that the head or senior staff imposed, but rather a self-development aspect, that reflected the teachers' own needs and desires to change their practice for themselves.

Collaborative partnership between schools and HEIs brings exciting new approaches to change. Change can be seen as proactive rather than reactive, by encouraging teachers to discuss ideas and proposals based on intrinsic merits or demerits of the proposals themselves, rather than personal likes and dislikes. Supportive environments such as these have encouraged teachers to take the types of risks that successful change involves. The fear of failure is no longer viewed as personally damning, but rather an experience to analyse, learn from and develop. The most positive aspect of school/HEI partnership is the nature of the change and development that occurs within the school context. Close collaboration enables the HEI to come into the school and become part of the school environment in such a way that teachers consider them to be 'insiders', non-threatening, supportive and open to ideas concerning the school's need to change and their own development. This ultimately increases teachers' sense of self-worth and professionalism and leads to a more effective school.

Collaboration through partnership encourages INSET at two levels; first, general skills and means-oriented activities which encourage and enable schools and teachers to obtain the necessary knowledge to start a programme of improvement; second, to support long-term development that allows teachers to increase personal knowledge and view change as a whole-school issue. This requires schools and HEIs to reconceptualize the problems associated with knowledge transmission, skills development and school improvement.

What can be Learnt from a Theoretical Perspective

Exploring social theories of institutional structures highlights areas such as trust, reflexivity, mutual knowledge, dialogue and the acknowledgement of differences.

Psychological theory gives us a perspective on knowledge construction and the learning process within a social context. Synthesizing the two contexts has produced areas that are conducive to collaboration and others that show significant weakness. If a collaborative framework is to be established and sustained the following need to be considered:

1. Differences in institutional cultures and structures are bound to produce conflict in sustained, substantive collaborations. Just as individual teachers and researchers bring to a collaboration different experiences, values and incentive systems for participation, so do the collaborating institutions. As with individuals, such institutional differences are important factors that will influence the direction the collaboration takes.
2. Collaboration requires a core working together and understanding how systems within institutional structures enable or constrain collaborative commitment.
3. Acknowledging difference in Dewey's terms is crucial to a collaborative framework.
4. Often a mismatch between HEIs' and schools' value systems is not conducive to a collaborative framework.
   (Cuban, 1992)

If collaboration is to succeed it needs to consider continual professional development as a construction of knowledge and learning, as well as an opportunity to connect research and practice. Sustained, substantive collaboration needs to be grounded in a sense of respectful, reflective equity among its participants. Equity must be apparent in both the institutional and personal-professional realities of the partnership. Understanding the participants within a partnership is essential to success. This has clearly been demonstrated in the two case studies.

Chapter 6

The Nature of Collaboration in the Future

How can we further develop collaborative partnership? In this final chapter the main features of collaboration will be reviewed and some possible future directions for collaborative ventures will be put forward.

The previous chapters have identified problematic areas and issues, but there have also emerged some distinct benefits, particularly when considering the continuum of professional development. Opportunities and barriers to development will be examined in the light of new government initiatives and the creation of the Teacher Training Agency (TTA).

There are two significant areas of partnership that have been highlighted throughout the book: ITE, in which schools and HEI have to work in a partnership that emphasizes their distinct but equally important contributions, and the provision of school-focused and school-based INSET. The latter is increasingly gaining recognition and approval as the way forward to continual professional development, with the added impetus of such courses gaining accreditation.

Of equal importance is the fact that the TTA is now making available funds for teachers to be actively involved in school-based research that will help pupil learning and individual teacher development. This can be viewed as a very positive move, contrary to many critics. It does appear that new opportunities and chances are being presented to schools and HEIs as a way of building and adapting existing good practice. Developments will be more successful if both institutions work in collaborative frameworks, as suggested in Chapter 3.

Through the exchange of ideas, expertise and practice, positive developments will occur that can only help extend the notion of good practice and valuable user-friendly research.

Developing Future Collaborations

It is inevitable that the schools and HEIs will remain in partnership with respect to the 'planning and management of training courses' (DES, 1992, Annex A). The nature of these partnership agreements will in essence depend on the nature of collaboration individual institutions wish to operate irrespective of government dictates and recommendations. The negotiation of roles and responsibilities will raise issues of generic and regional considerations. A system of partnership for one set of institutions may not be appropriate to another, but a collaborative framework based on trust, mutuality and equity does allow partnership agreements to state student entitlement, delineations between schools and HEIs, and assessment procedures and responsibilities.

The most significant aspect of Circular 9/92 (DfE, 1992) is that for many HEIs the introduction of ITE partnership has opened up opportunities for closer relationships and collaborative ventures between institutions. This has mainly concentrated on professional development of mentors, but institutions are, and have been, exploring school-based teacher research as a way of meeting individual development needs within a school development plan, by offering long-term, award-bearing projects.

These joint ventures, whether award-bearing or not, have been initiated and negotiated by representatives from both schools and HEIs, thus reinforcing the collaborative nature of the professional development. An example is the school-based curriculum development project described in the first case study in Chapter 4.

In some ways, the previous links with schools through ITE have facilitated such collaborative moves, and enabled both teacher and tutor opportunities for continual professional development through the sharing of expertise. Such partnerships are beneficial to both institutions. However, some schools may prefer more traditional working practices with respect to INSET and ITE, as they feel more at ease with 'tried and tested' systems. It is these institutions that need to consider the benefits and positive rewards that working collaboratively can bring for the school, teacher and pupil.

Undoubtedly there is in both ITE and school-based teacher research a shift in the power balance towards schools. Using Giddens' (1994) argument of 'choice', schools can choose to be in partnership for ITE, they can choose the nature of their INSET, they can choose whether they wish to be involved in collaborative research, in fact they can even stipulate if they want research undertaken for them. Schools are increasingly at the centre of their own development, and it is therefore crucial that future partnerships expose and exploit each institution's strengths if development is to continue.

Schools and HEIs are intrinsically involved with education, and actively enter into its constitution; they construct, support and change because it is in the nature of teachers and teacher educators to be affected by, and to affect, their social and educational environments. Teachers and teacher educators do not remain unmoved by their own feelings and motivations; they are not simply compelled by external forces, nor do they act mechanically or blindly. By reflecting on their behaviour and circumstances they always have choice. I would therefore like to suggest that to some degree, teachers and teacher educators are capable of resisting constraints imposed on them by government, TTA, school/HEI policies, etc, and of influencing and transforming their educational environment. This argument is based on Giddens' (1984) view of 'structuration'. He stresses that people are skilled and knowledgeable and are therefore not 'dupes' of the system or mere reflections or bearers of its demands and requirements.

If this is the case, it is of even greater importance for schools to choose to work with HEIs and vice versa. With the TTA giving research grants directly to teachers for school-based research, and pushing harder for greater school involvement in ITE, teachers and teacher educators have to make choices as to how and why these enforced changes are to be negotiated. Often schools and HEIs complement each other's initiatives, but change will only occur if both institutions genuinely collaborate by pooling expertise, rather than simply reflecting imposed structures and demands. Again, Giddens' (1994) argument helps here when considering future partnership development. He argues that structure is not external to action; it is, in a sense, more 'internal' to the flow of action which constitutes the practices in question.

This implies that teachers and teacher educators can create meaning and educational reality from the environmental settings they find themselves in; therefore institutions such as schools and HEIs have no existence apart from the activities they embody. However, whatever partnerships are established between institutions, consideration needs to be given to the manner in which individuals' reasons and intentions are centrally involved in the creation and re-creation of that partnership. This brings the argument for future developments back to choice.

As with any change or initiative leading to change, the process has to be well managed, and at a pace which allows for both individual and institutional development.

Establishing a collaborative approach to continuing professional development requires a shared understanding by both schools and HEIs; it will take time to implement and evaluate. It is a necessary prerequisite for quality education in the future. School-based teacher research and HEI research should be regarded as complementary not competitive; only then will partnership and equity develop.

Obstacles to Collaborative Initiatives

A major obstacle to collaborative initiatives has been, and often still is, the interpretation of 'collaboration'. It raises specific issues for institutions wishing to work together, concerned with the differences that distinguish one collaboration from another, and the multiple emerging roles within collaborative initiatives with respect to time, skills, expertise, commitment, cost and benefits. A frequent question is, 'Will a collaborative partnership produce a better product or outcome?' Understanding how the role of collaboration is seen in the learning and developmental processes is essential to overcoming the product/outcome obstacle.

Collaborations frequently encounter intellectual tension (Fullan, 1993; Hargreaves, 1994, 1995). These should not be regarded as obstacles but as a means of introducing new ideas. Dewey's (1934) notion of the 'problematic' allows us to consider intellectual tension as a means for explaining uncertainties found in problematic situations. Dewey considers this as essential to inquiry, and necessary when interpreting situations. The term 'problematic' does not relate to conflict; it is more one of experiencing tension when trying to understand differences of opinion.

Collaboration requires individuals to understand difference (Dewey) not only with respect to other individuals, but their own institution and other individuals and institutions. Therefore, trust is essential and necessary for collaborative projects. The nature of this trust must nourish dialogue and inquiry, allowing those involved in the collaboration to tolerate ambiguity, misunderstanding, a divergence of views and continuing discussions even when the situation is uncomfortable, without forcing collaborations into one position or another.

In view of the enforced changes schools and HEIs have had to endure and still endure, this discussion seems a distant reality. However, I feel that there is great scope for dialogue, and that there is a greater sense of equity between schools and HEIs than is actually suggested. Nevertheless, there are anxieties from both schools and HEIs about their future roles in teacher education and development. This is one area where the TTA has a crucial role to play.

Continual Professional Development and the Teacher Training Agency

The introduction of the TTA has caused many anxieties among teachers, teacher educators and their respective institutions. The TTA was set up as a quango responsible for all areas of teacher education. Its remit includes:

- funding and promotion of high quality teacher education;
- accreditation of providers of ITE;
- provision of information and advice about the teaching profession;

- funding classroom-based research;
- supporting CPD.

The TTA published its corporate plan in March 1995 stating that its main aim was to promote choice, diversity, efficiency and accountability throughout teacher education.

In her first public address, in February 1995, Anthea Millett, the TTA's Chief Executive, stressed the importance of partnership between schools and HEIs by highlighting the possibilities of increased and enhanced job satisfaction and a greater understanding of professional development needs through easier access to HEIs. She focused on the identification of issues within school improvement, increased opportunities for classroom-based research and the whole notion of the continuum of professional development. A key element of this speech was the need to develop and increase the status of professionalism of both teachers and their training.

The effect of the TTA to date

With respect to teachers' professional development and school-based research the TTA has spent £60,000 on research grants, awarding them to 33 teachers to carry out classroom research. The monies allocated can be used to buy supply cover to release the teachers for research, travel expenses, library work, and to buy tutorials from HEI staff. The types of research projects being funded range from 'comparisons of teaching styles in physical education to ways of improving nursery children's language using role play' (Parker, 1995).

The TTA has stated that these grants reflect the agency's commitment to developing teachers as a profession that is guided by high quality practical research. Geoffrey Parker, the agency's chairman, suggested that:

> 'Teachers are keen to have a bigger voice in what research gets done. They have a real contribution to make and these grants will help support their efforts. The projects we are funding go to the heart of the issue about how to improve the quality of teaching and learning in our schools. We shall start to see the benefits of the research by the end of this year and will begin to disseminate findings next spring.'

He takes his argument further in his speech when he discusses why these initiatives are so important to schools and individual teachers:

> 'Many teachers these days undertake research as part of a Masters degree but, unless there is a clear dissemination strategy, much of the value of the research is wasted.'

Where does this leave HEIs in terms of school-based research and the notion of collaborative partnership? At present this would seem tenuous. Geoffrey Parker's views on HEIs' contribution were also aired, indicating that:

'This is the first round of funds from the Agency for classroom-based research and we intend that there shall be many more over the years to come. I also believe that this initiative will be a further stimulus in the debate we continue to have with academic education researchers about the shortcomings of much traditional education research, which in our view is still too little focused on classroom teaching or on the messages needed for day to day classroom practice.'

This would appear to be a difficult time for HEIs as they contemplate the debate about what constitutes educational research and the role and useful-ness of its outcomes. Just prior to this book going to press, Professor David Hargreaves gave the TTA annual lecture on 'Teaching as a research-based profession: possibilities and prospects'. This lecture has sparked off a major educational debate, which is full of passion and division. The educational community now needs to come to a consensus if it is not to lose all school-based research to schools through the TTA; after all, schools' primary function is to teach pupils! Equally, the nature of the research being funded by the TTA would appear to be context-bound, with similar questions being asked about its dissemination.

The specification document for TTA school-based research funding (1996) makes interesting reading, for example:

- projects will need to be set in the context of TTA priorities (para. 19);
- teachers are expected to show a personal commitment by ensuring that the project is completed by drawing on their own personal time beyond the school day (para. 15);
- publication, in all cases, will need to be approved by the TTA (para. 22).

These statements strongly suggest that the TTA 'knows best', and will have a direct influence on what is researched and published. Will this approach be any more effective in developing and disseminating research that is of value to teachers in schools? Or is it merely a mirror image of what HEIs are presently being accused of?

Following Professor Hargreaves' lecture there will undoubtedly be consid-erable discussion, argument and rhetoric on these issues, particularly as part of the process of establishing, supporting and making credible any new approaches to teachers' professional development through research. Yet, seen in the context of existing collaborations between HEIs and schools, more open dialogue is required so that the diversity and potential of these collabo-rations is not only heard and seen, but also shown to be successful in the tasks they set out to accomplish. Very often these are exactly what the TTA is calling for: school improvement and enhanced professional development of the educational community.

The Need for Partnership

The TTA's view is that a knowledge base that underpins effective teaching is still in the process of being developed, whether this knowledge is derived through HEI or school-based teacher research. What needs to be considered is sustained continual professional development that will enhance and improve education. This applies to both schools and HEIs. Continuous development of all teachers is the cornerstone for meaning, improvement and reform. Professional development and school development are inextricably linked (Fullan, 1991, p.315).

This implies that teacher development depends on more than just the individual; it relies on all those involved in education. Fullan suggests that effective in-service education is characteristically underpinned by an understanding of what is to be achieved by INSET. Both teachers and teacher educators want to succeed in a way that not only enhances their personal knowledge but leads to effective change and improved learning. If Fullan's opinions are to be heeded, effective teacher development will only be accomplished through effective change processes. This is a major reason why partnership and especially collaborative partnerships need to be developed and encouraged. To make my point, I will take one of Fullan's examples of why in-service education has failed: 'there is a profound lack of any conceptual basis in the planning and implementing of in-service programmes that would ensure their effectiveness' (Fullan, 1979, p.3). If professional development is to improve learning outcomes and increase individuals' knowledge, then courses or projects in which they are engaged have to be relevant, stimulating, challenging and such that they can be implemented and disseminated within a school setting.

With the TTA suggesting school-based teacher research, school-focused INSET, school-based ITE and teacher professionalism, it raises the question of whether there is a role for HEIs in teacher education. It would seem that HEIs must evaluate how they can most effectively contribute to such endeavours and use them to take forward educational knowledge in collaboration with schools. Making explicit their findings and possible working structures that would facilitate the dissemination and implementation of collaborative work, can only be good for the development of all concerned. This will only occur if theirs is a joint conceptual understanding of what is to be planned, delivered, disseminated and implemented. HEIs can and are already beginning to have a distinctive role to play in the school improvement movement. By supporting improvement HEIs will have the ability and knowledge to research effectiveness. For too long they have concentrated on theoretical perspectives on what constitutes effectiveness. They are now in a position to develop improvement strategies collaboratively with schools, and then research how these alter the effectiveness of a school. Oakeshott's (1991) notion of civil association is the key to such partnership, ie, an understanding of difference depends on 'intelligent relationships' which respect each other's autonomy and accept different contexts.

At the beginning of this book I suggested that collaborative partnership between schools and HEIs could be a dynamic way of enhancing the quality of professional development, and that partnership in this mode must be regarded as a positive way of providing good, well-structured support for both the experienced and novice teacher. I suggest that it could be seen as a dynamic situation for improving personal knowledge, effective teaching situations and quality professional development in both institutions.

The challenge it offered was that expertise could be a two-way flow, whereby a dynamic equilibrium of professional interchanges could be created; that of continual exploration, enquiry, discussion, reflection, evaluation, action and support. Within this scenario, teacher educators and researchers could learn and develop from the expertise the teachers brought to the situation, and teachers could learn research strategies that would help active, systematic enquiry. In other words, teachers become part of the development/research environment, rather than being the 'subjects' of research.

In the light of TTA directives and current debates about school improvement and the role educational research has to play in it, much could be accomplished through mutual respect for the roles schools and HEIs have, and what each can contribute through their 'differences' and experiences. True collaborative partnership is the way forward to meeting the demands of an important educational forum. My hope is that such partnerships have the opportunity to develop and flourish, and that they will come to be seen as a way of increasing professionalism throughout education.

A Final Word

Changing educational ideas and attempting to change educational perspectives is not easy at any time (Cuban, 1990; Fullan, 1991; Sarason, 1990). It is particularly difficult when change involves a reconceptualization of roles and responsibilities within frameworks that have existed for a very long period of time and are often seen as immovable. Introducing new ideas and terms such as collaborative partnership, shared leadership and equity becomes increasingly difficult in an environment that does not want, or is frightened to accept collaborative partnership. In our work to date, eight significant obstacles to such change have been found:

1. definition of role that limits collaborative initiatives;
2. implicit and explicit conceptions of what it means to work as a professional within a given institution;
3. conceptions of what it is to learn professionally, both explicitly and implicitly;

4. career development: competition between colleagues for attention and prestige;
5. lack of understanding about institutional differences;
6. implicit and explicit hierarchical structures;
7. lack of common communicative language;
8. lack of understanding of the need to collaborate.

If these obstacles are not acknowledged and discussed, schools and HEI departments of education could find long-term changes occurring that are of no benefit to either. Throughout this book many examples have been given of how to make collaborative activities function within schools and HEIs. Improvement occurs only when action takes place. The sooner both institutions realize that 'action' is the key to effectiveness, and that collaborative partnership is the way forward, the sooner improvement will follow.

In view of the current debates about research applicability and funded teacher research being introduced in schools, it is now time to consider the roles and responsibilities of schools and HEI departments of education. Rigid role definitions are destructive and create barriers to institutional collaboration and the construction of professional work. Constructing professional work does not mean losing sight of what one is expected to do, but requires flexibility and an understanding of what it is to be involved in professional development. Undoubtedly interaction between HEI teacher educators and school teachers will involve a reconceptualization of what a university teacher educator's work involves, what a teacher's work involves and senior management's role in facilitating such changes.

If we are to see teacher education as a continuum of development, we need to recognize that ITE and CPD will increasingly be merging together. This may well require all of us in education to move away from the rigidity of our institutional expectations to a more collaborative view of what constitutes education and the role of development within that context. Such changes can be seen in the Annenberg model that Christelle described in Chapter 4. Collaborative partnership is essentially about changing the context for professional learning and development in education. Professional learning should be interactive, whereby experiences impact on individuals in such a way as to allow them to construct meaning for themselves, and as a consequence call on those meanings when necessary. Professional learning is both explicit and implicit, involving conceptual, social and emotional interactions. This again is very evident from the responses Christelle gained from her teachers, and those of my schools in England. Although each group articulated their fears and hopes in different terms, the ideas are fundamentally the same.

Hierarchical structures, personal and career developments, and institutional expectations appear to cause fundamental barriers to collaborative development. Hierarchical structures can be overcome by shared leadership, which would allow emerging ideas from schools and HEIs to be openly discussed and developed. Such shared leadership then allows research opportunities and training and development initiatives to co-exist. At the heart of collaborative partnership is the understanding and acceptance of 'difference' and 'intelligent relationships'.

'Whatever contributes to understanding also contributes to reconstruction.' (Willard Waller, 1967)

Bibliography

Annenbury Institute School Reform (AISR) (1995) Report, Boston, MA.

Argyris, C and Schön, D A (1974) *Theory into Practice: Increasing professional effectiveness*, San Francisco, CA: Jossey-Bass.

Argyris, C and Schön, D A (1978) *Organizational Learning: A theory of action perspectives*, Reading, MA: Addison-Wesley.

Bakhtin, M M (1981) 'Discourse in the novel', in Holquist, M (ed.) *The Dialogic Imagination* (pp.259–422), Austin, TX: University of Texas Press.

Bakhtin, M M (1986) *Speech Genes and Other Essays* (V McGee, trans. C Emerson and M Holquist, eds), Austin, TX: University of Texas Press.

Ball, S J (1987) *The Micro-politics of the School*, London: Methuen.

Batsleer, J, Randall, S and Paton, R (1992) *Environment and Strategy. Book 12 of OU course B789. Managing voluntary and non-profit enterprise*, Milton Keynes: Open University.

Bickel, W E and Hattrup, R A (1991–92) 'A case study of institutional collaboration to enhance knowledge use: restructuring practitioner-researcher dialogue in education', *Knowledge and Policy: The International Journal of Knowledge Transfer and Utilisation*, 4, 4, 56–78.

Bickel, W E and Hattrup, R A (1995) 'Teachers and researchers in collaboration: reflections on the process', *American Educational Research Journal*, 32, 1, 35–62.

Bidell, T (1988) 'Vygotsky, Piaget and the dialectic of development', *Human Development*, 31, 329–48.

Billing, M (1990) 'Stacking the cards of ideology: the history of the *Sun* souvenir Royal Album', *Discourse and Society*, 1, 17–38.

Billings, D E (1977) 'The nature and scope of staff development in institutions of higher education', in Elton, T and Simmonds, K (eds) *Staff Development in Higher Education*, Guilford: SRHE.

Bloom, A (1987) *The Closing of the American Mind: How higher education has failed democracy and impoverished the souls and minds of today's students*, New York: Simon & Schuster.

Bogden, R and Taylor, R (1975) *Introduction to Qualitative Research Methods: A phenomenological approach to the social sciences*, New York: John Wiley.

Bolam, R (1986) 'Conceptualising in-service', in Hopkins, D (ed.) *In-service Training and Educational Development: An institutional survey*, Beckenham: Croom Helm.

Bolam, R (1993) 'Recent developments and emerging issues', in *The Continuing Professional Development of Teachers*, General Teaching Council, England and Wales Trust, London: HMSO.

Bolam, R (1994) 'The impact of research on policy and practice in continuing professional development', *British Journal of In-service Education*, 20, 135–46.

Bolam, R (1995) 'The induction of newly qualified teachers in schools: where next?',
    British Journal of In-service Education, 21, 3, 247–60.
Bradley, H W (1991) *Staff Development*, London: Falmer Press.
Brand, A (1990) *The Force of Reason*, Sydney: Allen & Unwin.
Bridges, D (1993) 'School-based teacher education in developing teachers professionally',
    in Bridges, D and Kerry, T (eds), *Education in the Market Place*, London: Falmer Press.
Bruner, J (1989) *Actual Minds, Possible Words*, Cambridge, MA: Harvard Press.
Bullough, R V (1991) 'Exploring personal metaphors in pre-service teacher education',
    Journal of Teacher Education, 42, 1, 43–51.
Bullough, R V, Knowles, J G and Crow, N (1991) *Emerging as a Teacher*, London:
    Routledge.
Calhoun, E F and Glickman, D A (1993) 'Issues and dilemmas of action research in the
    league of professional schools', paper presented to the annual meeting of the
    American Educational Research Association (AERA), Atlanta, USA.
Canterbury Christ Church College (1992) *Portfolio of Curriculum Development Handbook*,
    Canterbury: CCCC.
Carr, W and Kemmis, S (1986) *Becoming Critical : Education, knowledge and action research*,
    London: Falmer Press.
Caulderhead, J (1983) 'Research into teachers' and student teachers' cognitions:
    exploring the nature of classroom practice', paper given at AERA, Montreal, Canada.
Clark, G (1991) *Dialogue, Dialectic and Conversation: A social perspective on the function of
    writing*, Carbondale, IL: Southern Illinois University Press.
Cornbleth, C (1986) 'Cries of crisis, calls for reform and challenges of change', in Weis, L,
    Altbach, R, Kelly, G, Petrie, H and Slaughter, S (eds) *Crisis in Teaching*, New York:
    State University of New York Press.
Corrie, L (1995) 'The structure and culture of staff collaboration: managing meaning and
    opening doors', *Educational Review*, 47, 89–100.
Cripseels, J (1992) *Purposeful Reconstructing*, London: Falmer Press.
Crozier, G (1990) 'Progressive and democratic education: is there a future?' *British Journal
    of Sociology*, 10, 2, 263–9.
Crozier, G, Menter, I and Pollard, A (1990) 'Changing Partnership', in Booth, M, Furlong,
    J and Wilkin, M (eds), *Partnership in Initial Teacher Training*, Cassell, London.
Cuban, L (1990) 'Reforming, again, again, and again', *Educational Researcher*, 19, 3–13.
Cuban, L (1992) 'Managing dilemmas while building communities', *Educational
    Researcher*, 21, 1, 4–11.
Daniels, H (1992) 'The individual and the organisation', in Daniels, H (ed.) *Charting the
    Agenda*, London: Routledge.
Davies, B and Harre, R (1990) 'Positioning: conversations and the production of selves',
    Journal for the Theory of Social Behaviour, 20, 43–63.
Day, C (ed.) (1986) *Staff Development in the Secondary School: Management perspectives*,
    Beckenham: Croom Helm.
Day, C (1993a) Inaugural lecture: 'Research and the continuing professional
    development of teachers', University of Nottingham.
Day, C (1993b) 'Reflection: a necessary but not sufficient condition for professional
    development', *British Educational Research Journal*, 19, 1, 83–93.
Day, C (1995) 'Qualitative research, professional development and the role of teacher
    educators: fitness for purpose', *British Educational Research Journal*, 21, 357–70.
Day, C and Pennington, A C (1993) 'Conceptualising professional development
    planning: a multidimensional model', *International Analyses of Teacher Education, JET
    papers one*, Abingdon: Carfax.

Day, C et al. (1987) *Appraisal and Professional Development in Primary Schools*, Buckingham: Open University Press.

Dean, J (1991) *Professional Development in School*, Buckingham: Open University Press.

Dearing, Sir Ron (1994) *The National Curriculum and its Assessment*, London: SCAA.

Denzin, N K (1987) *The Research Act: A theoretical introduction to sociological methods*, New York: McGraw-Hill.

DES (1972) *Teacher Education and Training* (The James Report), London: HMSO.

DES (1984) *Statistics of Education: Teachers in service, England and Wales*, London: HMSO.

DES (1986) *Local Education Authority Training Grant Scheme, 1987–88*. Circular 6/86, London: HMSO.

DES (1987) *School Teachers' Pay and Conditions of Employment*. Circular 40/87, London: HMSO.

DES (1989) *Initial Teacher Training: Approval of courses*. Circular 24/89, London: HMSO.

DfE (1992) *Initial Teacher Training: Secondary phase*. Circular 9/92, London: HMSO.

DfE (1993a) *Initial Teacher Training: Primary school teachers, new criteria for courses*. Circular 14/93, London: HMSO.

DfE (1993b) *The Government's Proposals for the Reform of Initial Teacher Training*, London: HMSO.

Dewey, J (1916) *Democracy and Education*, Basingstoke: Macmillan.

Dewey, J (1934) *How we Think*, Boston, MA: Heath.

Elliott, J (1991) *Action Research for Educational Change*, Buckingham: Open University Press.

Elliott, J (1994) 'Research on teacher's knowledge and action research', *Educational Action Research*, 2, 133–40.

Elliott, J, Bridges, D, Ebutt, D, Gibson, R and Nias, J (1981) *Schools' Accountability*, London: Grant MacIntyre.

Eraut, M (1987) *Local Evaluation of INSET: A meta evaluation of TRIST evaluation*, Bristol: National Development Centre for School Management.

Eraut, M and Holyes, C (1989) 'Group work with computers', *Journal of Computer Assisted Learning*, 5, 12–24.

Feiman-Nemser, S and Floden, R E (1986) 'The cultures of teaching', in Wittrock, M C (ed.) *Handbook of Research on Teacher Thinking* (3rd edn), New York: Macmillan.

Fullan, M (1979) *School-focused In-service Education in Canada*, report for the Centre of Educational Research and Innovation, Paris: OECD.

Fullan, M (1985) 'Change process and strategies at the local level', *The Elementary Journal*, 84, 3, 391–420.

Fullan, M (1990) 'Staff development, innovation and institutional development', in Joyce, B (ed.) *Changing School Culture through Staff Development*, Alexandria, VA: ASCD.

Fullan, M (1991) *The New Meaning of Educational Change*, London: Cassell.

Fullan, M (1993) *Change Forces: Probing the depths of educational reform*, London: Falmer Press.

Fullan, M and Hargreaves, A (1991) *What's Worth Fighting for in Your School?* Buckingham: Open University Press.

Fullan, M G and Stieglbauer, S (1991) *The New Meaning of Educational Change* (2nd edn), New York: Teachers College Press

Gallacher, N (1995) 'Partnership in education', in Macbeth, A, McCreath, D and Aitchison, J (eds) *Collaborate or Compete*, London: Falmer Press.

Garrison, J (1995) 'Deweyan pragmatism and social constructivism', *American Educational Research Journal*, 3, 4, 716–40.

Gee, J (1990) *Social Linguistics and Literacies: Ideology in discourse*, London: Falmer Press.

Geertz, C (1973) 'From the native's point of view: on the nature of anthropological understanding', in Rainbow, P and Sullivan W (eds) *Interpretative Social Science: A reader*, Berkeley, CA: University of California Press.

Giddens, A (1984) *The Constitution of Society*, Cambridge: Polity Press.

Giddens, A (1989) *Sociology*, Cambridge: Polity Press.

Giddens, A (1994) *Beyond Left and Right* (1st edn), Cambridge: Polity Press.

Giddens, A (1995) *Beyond Left and Right* (2nd edn), Cambridge: Polity Press.

Giddens, A (1996) *Politics, Sociology and Social Theory*, Cambridge: Polity Press.

Giroux, H and Freire, P (1988) 'Introduction', in Weiller, K, *Women Teaching for Change*, New York: Bergin & Garvey.

Glaser, B G and Strauss, A L (1967) *The Discovery of Grounded Theory*, Chicago, IL: Adine.

Goodlad, J E (1983) 'The school as workplace', in Griffin, G A (ed.) *Staff Development, 82nd Yearbook*, Chicago, IL: National Society for the Study of Education.

Goodlad, J E (1993) 'School-university partnership and partnership schools', *Educational Policy*, 7, 1, 24–39.

Goodson, I F (1992) 'Sponsoring the teacher's voice', in Hargreaves, A and Fullan, M (eds) *Understanding Teacher Development*, London: Cassell.

Greeno, J G (1989) 'A perspective on thinking', *American Psychologist*, 44, 134–41.

Grene, M (ed.) (1969) *Knowing and Being: Essays by Michael Polanyi*, Chicago, IL: University of Chicago Press.

Griffiths, M and Tann, S (1991) 'Ripples in the reflection', *BERA Dialogues*, 5, 82–101.

Grundy, S (1994) *Curriculum: Product or Praxis*, London: Falmer Press.

Habermas, J (1971a) *Knowledge and Human Interests* (trans. by S Shapiro), Boston, MA: Beacon Press.

Habermas, J (1971b) *Towards a Rational Society*, Oxford: Heinemann.

Handal, G (1991) 'Promoting the articulation of tacit knowledge through the counselling of practitioners', in Letiche, H K, Van Der Wolde, J C and Ploou, F X (eds), *The Practitioners' Power of Choice in Staff Development and INSET*, Amsterdam: Swets & Zeitinger.

Hargreaves, A (1983) 'The occupational culture of teachers', in Woods, P (ed.) *Teacher Strategies*, Beckenham: Croom Helm.

Hargreaves, A (1991) *Culture of Teaching*, London: Cassell.

Hargreaves, A (1993) 'Cultures of teaching: a focus for change in understanding teacher development', in Hargreaves, A and Fullan, M (eds), *Understanding Teacher Development*, London: Cassell.

Hargreaves, A (1994) *Changing Teachers, Changing Times: Teachers' work and cultures in the postmodern age*, London: Cassell.

Hargreaves, A (1995) 'Towards a social geography of teacher education', in Shimahard, N K and Holowinsky, I Z (eds) *Teacher Education in Industrialized Nations: Issues in changing social contexts*, New York: Garland.

Harland, J (1990) *The Work and Impact of Advisory Teachers*, Slough: NFER.

Harland, J and Kinder, K (1991) *The Impact of INSET: The case of primary science*, Slough: NFER.

Harre, R (1986) 'The step to social constructionism', in Richards, M and Light, P (eds), *Children of Social Worlds*, Cambridge: Polity Press.

Harre, R and Secord, P F (1972) *The Explanation of Social Behaviour*, Oxford: Basil Blackwell & Mott.

Henderson, J (1992) 'Curriculum discourse and the question of empowerment', *Theory into Practice*, 31, 204–9.

Hewton, E (1989) *School-focused Staff Development*, London: Falmer Press.

HMI (1988) *A Critique of the Implementation of the Cascade Model Used to Provide INSET for Teachers in Preparation for the Introduction of the General Certificate of Secondary Education*, London: DES.

Hopkins, D (1987) *Improving the Quality of Schooling*, London: Falmer Press.

Hoyle, E (1973) 'Strategies for curriculum change', in Watkins, R (ed.) *In-service Training: Structures and content*, London: Ward Lock.

Hoyle, E (1974) 'Professionality, professionalism and control in teaching', *Educational Review*

Jackson, P W (1968) *Life in Classrooms*, New York: Holt, Rinehart and Winston.

Johnson, D and Johnson, R (1985) 'Cooperative learning: one key to computer-assisted learning', *Computing Teacher*, 13, 11–13.

Johnson, M *et al.* (1996) 'Defining and negotiating leadership roles', paper presented at AERA, Atlanta, USA.

Johnston, S and Hedemann, M (1994) 'School level curriculum decisions – a case of battling against the odds', *Educational Review*, 46, 3.

Joyce, L (1989) 'Staff development as cultural change', paper presented at the international conference of the Hong Kong Educational Research Association, November.

Lieberman, A (1989) *Building a Professional Culture in Schools*, New York: Teachers College Press.

Lieberman, A (1992) 'The meaning of scholarly activity and the building of community', *Educational Researcher*, 21, 6, 5–12.

Lincon, Y S (1992) 'Systematic connections between qualitative methods and health research', *Qualitative Health Research*, 2, 375–92.

Lincon, Y S and Guba, E G (1985) *Naturalistic Inquiry*, Beverly Hills, CA: Sage.

Little, J W (1990) 'The persistence of privacy: autonomy and initiative in teachers' professional relations', *Teachers College Record*, 91, 4, 509–36.

Lortei, D C (1975) *Schoolteacher: A Sociological Study*, Chicago, IL: Chicago University Press.

Loucks-Horsley, S *et al.* (1987) *Continuing to Learn: A guidebook for teacher development*, Andover: Regional Laboratory for Educational Improvement of the Northeast Island National Staff Development Council.

Louden, W R (1992) 'Understanding reflection through collaboration', in Hargreaves, A and Fullan, M (eds) *Understanding Teacher Development*, London: Cassell.

Lytle, S L and Cochran-Smith, M (1990) 'Learning form teacher research: a working typology', *Teachers College Record*, 92, 1, 83–103.

Lytle, S L and Cochran-Smith, M (1992) 'Communities for teacher researchers: fringe or forefront?', *American Journal of Education*, 100, 3, 298–324.

McCaslin, M and Good, T (1992) 'Complaint cognition: the misalliance of management and constructional goals in current school reform', *Educational Researcher*, 22, 7, 4–17.

McLaughlin, M W and Talbert, J E (1993) *Contexts that Matter for Teaching and Learning*, Stanford, CA: Center for Research on the Context of Secondary School Teaching.

McNeil, L (1989) 'Exit, voice and community', in Weis, L, Altbach, R, Kelly, G, Petrie, H and Slaughter, S (eds) *Crisis in Teaching*, Albany, NY: SUNY Press.

McNiff, J (1993) *Teaching and Learning*, London: Routledge.

McPherson, R B, Crowson, R L and Pitner, N J (1986) *Managing Uncertainty: Administrative theory and practice in education*, Columbus, OH: Charles Merrill.

Mezirow, J (1981) 'A critical theory of adult learning and education', *Adult Education*, 32, 1, 3–24.

Miles, M and Huberman, A (1984) *Qualitative Data Analysis. A source book of new methods*, Beverly Hills, CA: Sage.

Miller, J L (1990) *Creating Spaces and Finding Voices: Teachers collaborating for empowerment*, Albany, NY: SUNY Press.

Mishler, E G (1986) *Research Interviewing. Context and narrative*, Cambridge, MA: Harvard University Press.

Moore, M E (1991) *Teaching from the Heart: Theology and educational method*, Minneapolis: Minneapolis Press.

Nias, J (1989) *Primary Teachers Talking*, London: Routledge & Kegan Paul.

Nias, J (1991) 'How practitioners are silenced, how practitioners are empowered', in Letiche, H K, Van Der Wolde, J C and Ploou, F X (eds), *The Practitioners' Power of Choice in Staff Development and INSET*, Amsterdam: Swets & Zeitinger.

Nias, J, Southworth, G and Yeoman, R (1989) *Staff Relationships in the Primary School: A study of organisational structures*, London: Cassell.

Nicholls, G (1993) 'School-based teacher development: a research project', paper presented at International Conference of the Association of Teacher Education in Europe, Lisbon.

Nicholls, G (1994) 'School-based teacher development: the way ahead!', in Valente, A O and Barrios, A (eds) *Teacher Training and Values in Education*, Lisbon: University of Lisbon Press.

Nicholls, G (1995) 'School-based professional development: an experiment in long-term professional development', paper presented at International Conference for Teacher Research. University of California Davis, USA.

Oakeshott, M (1991) *On Human Conduct*, Oxford: Clarendon Press.

OFSTED (1993) *The New Teacher in School*, London: OFSTED.

OHMCI (1993) Office of Her Majesty's Chief Inspectorate, Report, HMSO: London.

Parker, G (1995) Press release from the TTA, 5 July. Extract cited in *Research Intelligence*, July, 57, 32.

Pennington, A (1994) 'Personal content knowledge in continuing professional development', *British Journal of Education*, 20, 3, 397–405.

Perry, P (1977) Keynote address to OECD/CERI International Workshop on School-focused INSET, West Palm Beach.

Piaget, J (1926) *The Language and Thought of the Child*, New York: Harcourt Brace Jovanovich.

Piaget, J (1928) *Judgement and Reasoning in the Child*, London: Routledge & Kegan Paul.

Polanyi, M (1958) *Personal Knowledge: Towards a post-critical philosophy*, Chicago, IL: University of Chicago Press.

Polanyi, M (1967) *The Tacit Dimension*, Chicago, IL: University of Chicago Press.

Potter, J and Wetherell, M (1987) *Discourse and Social Psychology*, London: Sage.

Pugach, M and Pasch, S (1992) 'The challenge of creating urban professional development schools', paper presented at the annual meeting of the AERA, San Francisco.

Pugh, G (1989) 'Parents and professionals in pre-school service: is partnership possible?' in Wolfendale, S (ed.) *Parental Involvement*, London: Cassell.

Rein, N and White, S M (1980) *Knowledge for Practice: The study of knowledge in context for practice of social work*, working paper for study in Research in Education, MIT, USA.

Resnick, L, Bickel, W E and Leinhardt, G (1987) *Proposal to the National Science Foundation: Disseminating new knowledge about mathematics instruction*, a collaborative project of the American Federation of Teachers and the Learning Research and Development Center, Learning and Development Center, Pittsburgh, PA.

Rogoff, B and Lave, J (eds) (1984) *Everyday Cognition*, Cambridge, MA: Harvard University Press.

Rousseau, J J (1979) *Emile or On Education* (trans. A Bloom), New York: Basic Books.

Ruddock, J (1987) 'Partnership supervision as a basis for the professional development of new and experienced teachers', in Wideen, M F and Andrews, I (eds) *Staff Development for School Improvement: A focus on the teacher*, London: Falmer Press.

Ruddock, J (1992) 'Universities in partnership with schools and school systems: *Les liaisons dangereuses?*, in Fullan, M and Hargreaves, A (eds) *Teacher Development and Educational Change*, London: Falmer Press.

Rutherford, W (1985) 'School principals as effective leaders', *Phi Delta Kappa*, 67, 31–4.

Sarason, S (1982) *The Culture of the School and the Problem of Change* (rev. edn) Boston: Allyn & Bacon.

Sarason, S (1990) *The Predictable Failure of Educational Reform*, San Francisco, CA: Jossey-Bass.

Schlechty, P C and Whitford, B L (1988) 'Shared problems and shared visions: organic collaboration', in Sirotnik, K A and Goodland, J I (eds) *School–university Partnerships in Action: Concepts, cases and concerns*, New York: Teachers College Press.

Schön, D A (1983a) *Educating the Reflective Practitioner* (1st edn), New York: Basic Books.

Schön, D A (1983b) *The Reflective Practitioner: How professionals think in action*, New York: Basic Books.

Schön, D A (1987) *Educating the Reflective Practitioner* (2nd edn), San Francisco, CA: Jossey-Bass.

Semin, G (1986) 'The individual, the social, and the social individual', *British Journal of Social Psychology*, 25, 3, 35–46.

Senge, P (1990) *The Fifth Discipline*, New York: Doubleday.

Shibutanti, T (1961) *Society and Personality*, Englewood Cliffs, NJ: Prentice Hall.

Shotter, J (1992) 'A sense of place: Vico and the social production of social identities', *British Journal of Social Psychology*, 25, 199–211.

Sirotnik, K A and Goodland, J I (eds) (1988) *School-university Partnerships in Action: Concepts, cases and concerns*, New York: Teachers College Press.

Slavin, P (1987) 'Development and motivational perspectives on conceptual learning: a reconciliation', *Child Development*, 56, 1161–7.

Stacey, R (1992) *Managing the Unknowable*, San Francisco, CA: Jossey-Bass.

Stoddart, T, Winitzky, N and O'Keefe, P (1992) 'Developing the professional development of school', paper presented at the annual meeting of AERA, San Francisco, CA.

Tarini, E (1993) 'Reflections, innovations in early education', *The International Reggio Exchange*, 1, 3, 4–5.

Tikunoff, W J, Ward, B and Griffen, G A (1979) *Interactive Research and Development on Teaching Study* (final report), San Francisco, CA: Far West Laboratory for Educational Research.

TTA (1996) *Continual Professional Development*, London: TTA.

Van Dijk, T (1990) 'Discourse and society: a new journal for research focus', *Discourse and Society*, 1, 5–17 .

Van Velzen, W et al. (1985) *Making School Improvement Work*, Leuven: ACCO.

Veal, I et al. (1989) 'School contexts that encourage reflection: teacher perceptions', *International Journal of Qualitative Studies in Education*, 2, 315–33.

Vygotsky, L S (1962) *Thought and Language*, Cambridge, MA: MIT Press.

Vygotsky, L S (1986) *Thought and Language* (trans. A Kozulin, ed.) Cambridge, MA: MIT Press.

Wahlstrom, K L and King, J A (1993) 'Emerging issues in collaborative action research at the Center for Applied Research and Educational Improvement', paper presented at the annual meeting of AERA, Atlanta, USA.

Waller, W (1967) *The Sociology of Teaching*, New York: John Wiley.

Watson, G (1976) 'A caring community: staff development in the school', *Secondary Education*, 6, 1, 20.

Watson, N and Fullan, M (1992) *Teacher Development and Educational Change*, London: Falmer Press.

Webb, C (1994) 'Working towards a school staff development policy', dissertation submission for Diploma in Curriculum Development, Canterbury Christ Church College.

Wise, A, Darling-Hammond, L, McLaughlin, M W and Bernstein, H (1985) 'Teacher evaluation: A study of effective practices', *The Elementary School Journal*, 86, 1, 61–121.

Young, R E (1993) *A Critical Theory of Education: Habermas and our children's future*, New York: Teachers College Press.

Zeichner, K (1993) 'Connecting genuine teacher development to the struggle for social justice', *Journal of Education for Teaching*, 19, 5–19.

Index